The **Button** CRAFT BOOK

Art Director: Dana Irwin
Photography: Evan Bracken, Light Reflections
Production: Elaine Thompson, Dana Irwin
Illustrations: Olivier Rollin
Proofreading: Julie Brown

Library of Congress Cataloging-in-Publication Data
Available

10 9 8 7 6 5 4 3 2 1

A Sterling/Lark Book

First paperback edition published in 1996 by
Sterling Publishing Company, Inc.
387 Park Avenue South, New York, N.Y. 10016

Produced by Altamont Press, Inc.
50 College Street, Asheville, NC 28801

© 1995 by Altamont Press

Distributed in Canada by Sterling Publishing
  c/o Canadian Manda Group, One Atlantic Avenue, Suite 105
  Toronto, Ontario, Canada M6K 3E7
Distributed in Great Britain and Europe by Cassell PLC
  Wellington House, 125 Strand, London WC2R 0BB, England
Distributed in Australia by Capricorn Link (Australia) Pty Ltd.
  P.O. Box 6651, Baulkham Hills, Business Centre, NSW 2153, Australia

Every effort has been made to ensure that all the information in this book is
accurate. However, due to differing conditions, tools, and individual skills, the
publisher cannot be responsible for any injuries, losses, and other damages which
may result from the use of the information in this book.

Printed in Hong Kong

Sterling ISBN 0-8069-3197-3 Trade
        0-8069-3198-1 Paper

The **Button**
CRAFT BOOK

Dawn Cusick

Sterling Publishing Co., Inc.   New York
A STERLING/LARK BOOK

TABLE
OF
CONTENTS

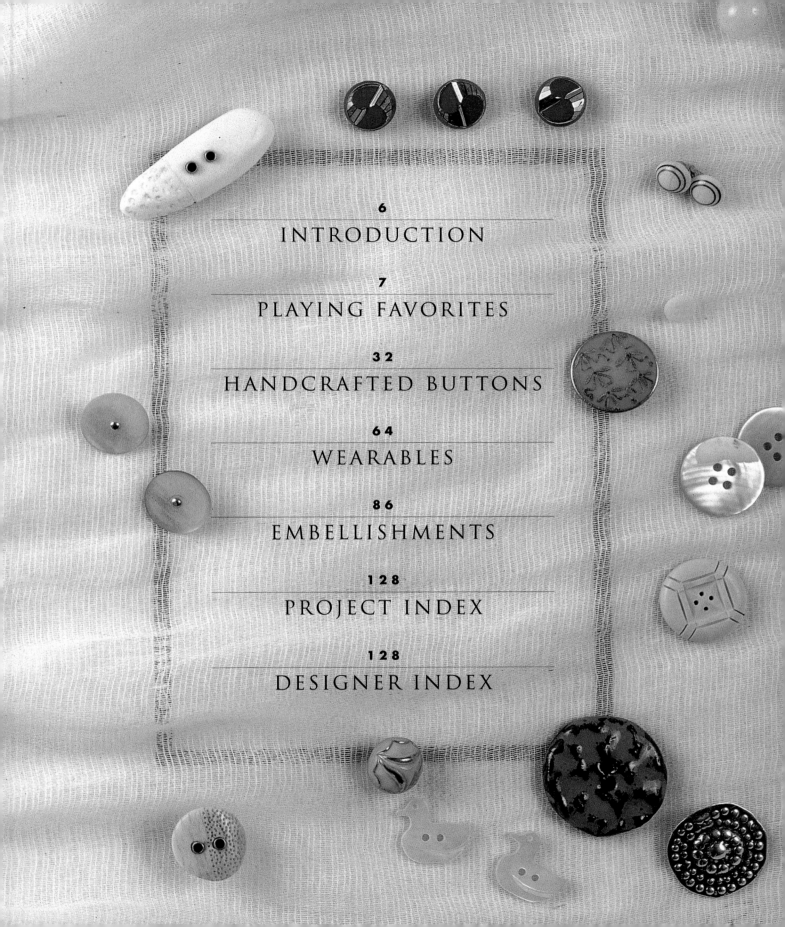

INTRODUCTION

Since the earliest days of civilization, there have been people who take joy in life's details and people who never even see them. The earliest buttons — dating back to 2000 B.C. if you believe the history books — were purely practical, simple closures designed to keep out the elements. Fortunately, it didn't take long for some keen individual to see a potential duality in buttons, a way to add art to something ordinary and necessary, and today, as all those hundreds of years ago, there are still those who see beauty in small details such as buttons. Button lovers, by their nature, appreciate subtlety, and the handcrafts they make are treasures to be discovered and rediscovered.

Developing a book about buttons has its obvious pleasures . . . my window sills are heaped high with gorgeous buttons . . . traffic jams have lost their familiar annoyance (I fantasize about replacing all my old buttons with spectacular ones) . . . and I've spent many guilt-free hours sifting through jars of special buttons. Developing a book about buttons also has its drawbacks. For all the treasures in this book, there are hundreds more that remain undiscovered, and that thought carries with it a sadness that's hard to shake.

If you're accustomed to step-by-step project instructions, you may initially feel some disappointment with this book. For the majority of the projects, though, the how-to techniques are as simple as gluing or sewing buttons. What makes these projects special is the imagination, the care, and the loving touch that went into creating them. The reasons designers chose particular buttons and materials are far more interesting (and ultimately much better learning tools) than whether the button in the top left quadrant is 5/8" or 7/8" and whether upholstery or quilting thread was used to sew it on. Use the projects as inspirations; feel free to adapt or recreate them, allowing your own special buttons to dictate materials and techniques. And always keep in mind that when you're working with a material as intrinsically charming as buttons, the finished pieces will always be a success.

PLAYING FAVORITES

Initially, a section profiling people's favorite buttons seemed like a wonderful idea. Traditional button histories have been done (and done well) by many others, and this seemed like a fun variation, a voyeuristic peek into the minds and collections of fellow button lovers. As we all know, though, not everything in life works out as planned. Requests for favorite buttons were frequently answered with long silences, exasperated sighs, and even great roars of laughter. It turns out that people who love buttons find it virtually impossible to choose just one, and respondents often sent a handful of buttons with notes that read, "Here are several of my favorites — you choose, because I can't" and the like. So as you browse through this chapter, think well of the people who forced themselves to choose a single favorite button, and ask yourself if you could do the same.

"My favorite buttons are the ones I've made from polymer clay. The medium is like magic . . . you never quite know what you're going to get when you mix the colors, and the serendipity of it just fits my personality.

"During the year I editored the PolyinforMer Newsletter, I heard from a lot of people who make buttons. My favorite was a woman from New Zealand who was selling hand-knit sweaters with handmade polymer clay buttons. A large knitting company was suing her because they believed they had exclusive rights to polymer clay buttons. I wrote an article entitled 'Button, Button, Who Can Make A Button?' and many of the national guild members became 'button activists.' We sent copies of clay button how-to articles and many members sent actual buttons to be entered as evidence. The woman finally won, and we really enjoyed helping her."

CINDY McILWAIN ■ RECENTLY RETIRED EDITOR ■ PolyinforMer Newsletter

"THE TASK OF
SELECTING MY FAVORITE
BUTTON WAS DAUNTING.
I CAN ONLY NARROW IT

**"MY LOVE OF BUTTONS HAS BEEN A FOCAL POINT
ON VIRTUALLY ALL OF MY OVERSEAS TRIPS."**

DOWN TO FOUR. MY LOVE
OF BUTTONS HAS BEEN A
FOCAL POINT ON VIRTUALLY
ALL OF MY OVERSEAS TRIPS.
THE BUTTONS MAKE WON-
DERFUL MEMENTOS AND
THEY DON'T TAKE UP MUCH
SPACE.

"THIS CUT-STEEL
BUTTON WAS PIVOTAL IN MY
BUTTON COLLECTION. IT WAS
PART OF THE FIRST GROUP
THAT I'VE ACTIVELY COLLECT-
ED. I HAD TAKEN SOME JEW-
ELRY COURSES AND I SAW
THIS AS A WONDERFUL CEN-
TERPIECE FOR 'SOMETHING.'
IT HANGS ON A RIBBON IN
MY STUDIO AS INSPIRATION."

AILEEN GUGENHEIM ■ OWNER, DESIGN SPECIALTIES

"I HAVE TWO BUTTONS THAT STAND OUT AS FAVORITES. ONE IS AN ANTIQUE BRASS PIG BUTTON

"I SEWED IT ONTO ONE OF MY HUSBAND'S SHIRT COLLARS AND FRAMED IT SO I COULD ENJOY IT EVERY DAY. "

THAT WAS A PRESENT FROM A CANADIAN FRIEND WHO KNEW I HAD A PIG COLLECTION IN MY KITCHEN. I SEWED IT ONTO ONE OF MY HUSBAND'S SHIRT COLLARS AND FRAMED IT SO I COULD ENJOY IT EVERY DAY.

"MY OTHER FAVORITE BUTTON IS A CROCHETED BUTTON FROM THE '30S. I HAD CARRIED IT AROUND WITH ME FOR AGES, LOOKING FOR A MATE TO IT. FINALLY, I GAVE UP AND USED IT AS THE CENTER BUTTON ON A SPECIAL FOOTSTOOL. OF COURSE, A MATCH TO THE BUTTON TURNED UP RIGHT AFTER THAT, SO NOW I HAVE TO MAKE ANOTHER FOOTSTOOL!"

DIANE WEAVER ■ CRAFT AUTHOR

"MY FAVORITE BUTTON, A BRASS BUTTON PICTURING A RABBIT AND A JACK-IN-THE-BOX, IS FROM THE 1800S. IT REMINDS ME OF MY CHILDHOOD PET RABBIT, WHICH WAS AS MUCH A PART OF MY DAILY LIFE AS MY TOYS. MOST OF MY BUTTON COLLECTION HAS BEEN ACQUIRED THROUGH REMINDERS OF MY PERSONAL LIFE. FOR EXAMPLE, I ENJOY BUTTONS WITH OAK LEAVES AND ACORNS BECAUSE I'VE LIVED ON AN OAK STREET AS A CHILD IN BOTH PENNSYLVANIA AND MICHIGAN. ONE OF MY BRASS BUTTONS FEATURES A BLACKSMITH'S SHOP AND REMINDS ME OF STORIES OF MY GREAT GRANDFATHER'S PROFESSION. LATELY, I'VE ACQUIRED SOME BEAUTIFUL BIRD BUTTONS, PARTIALLY DUE TO MY PET BUDGIES!

"I DISPLAY THE BUTTONS AROUND MY HOME, SOME INSIDE A GLASS-TOP TABLE AND

"MOST OF MY BUTTON COLLECTION HAS BEEN ACQUIRED THROUGH REMINDERS OF MY PERSONAL LIFE."

OTHERS STACKED IN A GROUPING OF PRINTER'S CABINET DRAWERS. THEY ALWAYS ENCHANT MY GUESTS, AND IT'S FUN TO WATCH THEM PICK UP THE TREASURES FOR CLOSER INSPECTION."

JAN KOZMA ■ SHOP MANAGER ■ RENAISSANCE BUTTONS

"FOR THE MOMENT, A SET OF CARVED HORN BUTTONS DISCOVERED IN A SPECIALTY YARN SHOP IS MY FAVORITE. I HAVE NOTHING TO GO WITH THEM, BUT THE LOGICAL SOLUTION IS TO KNIT SOMETHING. FALLING IN LOVE WITH A BUTTON AND THEN HAVING TO DESIGN A GARMENT OR AN ENTIRE OUTFIT TO GO ALONG WITH IT IS ONE OF MY FAVORITE BAD HABITS. 'MIGRATING BUTTONS' (MOVING THEM FROM ONE OUTFIT TO ANOTHER) IS ANOTHER IRRESISTIBLE HABIT. I'VE MOVED ONE SET OF ANTIQUE TORTOISE SHELL BUTTONS FROM FIVE OR SIX DIFFERENT OUTFITS OVER THE LAST 15 YEARS."

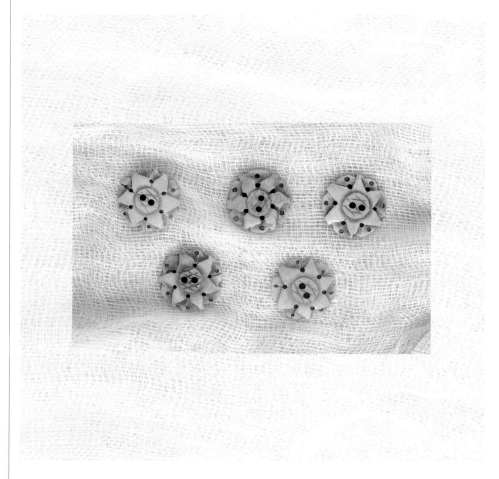

"FALLING IN LOVE WITH A BUTTON AND THEN HAVING TO DESIGN A GARMENT OR AN ENTIRE OUTFIT TO GO ALONG WITH IT IS ONE OF MY FAVORITE BAD HABITS. "

CAROL PARKS ■ SEWING AUTHOR

"My favorite buttons are from very special people. I cut the small button from David

"I CUT THE SMALL BUTTON FROM DAVID LETTERMAN'S DRESS SHIRT WHEN I DID AN APPEARANCE ON HIS SHOW."

Letterman's dress shirt when I did an appearance on his show. The other two buttons are from Senators Strom Thurmond and Ernest Hollins." Note: Dalton has a large number of buttons to choose favorites from. His personal hearse (see page 90) has more than 600,000 buttons on it.

Dalton Stevens ■ a.k.a., The Button King

"I FIND BUTTONS IRRE-SISTIBLE. MY FAVORITES ARE ON A FAIR ISLE SWEATER KNIT WITH 13 YARN COLORS. I COULDN'T FIND BUTTONS FOR IT ANYWHERE BECAUSE THE COLORS WERE SO UNUSUAL. IT WAS AMAZING: IT TOOK SIX WEEKS TO KNIT THE SWEATER AND SIX MONTHS TO FIND THE PER-FECT BUTTONS! MY HUS-BAND AND I FINALLY WENT DOWN TO TENDER BUTTONS AND DISCOVERED SOME HANDCRAFTED SILVER BUT-TONS FROM THE TURN OF THE CENTURY. WHEN I WEAR THE SWEATER TO A KNITTING CONFERENCE, THE FIRST THING MOST KNITTERS SAY IS, 'WHERE DID YOU GET THOSE BUTTONS?'

"I'M THRILLED TO SEE SUCH AN INTEREST IN HANDCRAFTED BUTTONS. GLASS BUTTONS, BEADED BUTTONS, AND COIN BUTTONS SEEM ESPECIALLY POPULAR AT THE

MOMENT. THERE'S ALSO A RESURGENCE OF INTEREST IN FINE-QUALITY SPECIALTY BUTTONS."

"IT TOOK SIX WEEKS TO KNIT THE SWEATER AND SIX MONTHS TO FIND THE PERFECT BUTTONS!"

ALICE KORACH ■ EDITOR ■ BEAD & BUTTON

"Most people collect buttons for their function or form. I collect them in remembrance. To me, each button is like a tiny time machine, taking me back to my grandparents' farmhouse. As a grandchild-in-residence (we lived next door), I visited often. Like many children, I was fascinated by buttons. I would stand in the middle of the kitchen staring up at the collection of button-filled mason jars, and Nana would say, 'Well, which one is it today?' I

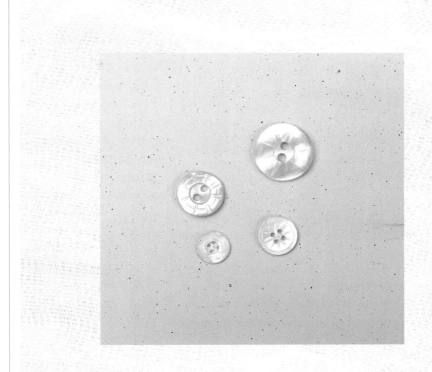

"TO ME, EACH BUTTON IS LIKE A TINY TIME MACHINE, TAKING ME BACK TO MY GRANDPARENTS' FARMHOUSE."

would pull my chair up to one of her large, enamel work tables and we would empty out the contents.

"My creativity blossomed on that work table as I made button jewelry, button boxes, and buttonscapes. My grandmother's favorites were buttons made of mother-of-pearl. She would pick each one up and hold it a minute before telling me about it. Most of the buttons had come from clothing worn by my mother and her sisters as children, and the buttons seemed to transport my grandmother back in time. Today, I too have amassed my own set of mason jars filled to capacity with my grandmother's and my favorite buttons, mother-of-pearl."

JUDITH STOLL

15

■ DECISIONS, DECISIONS

Left: Benjamin Blumenthal President 1877–1897

Below: J. & A. Blumenthal, brothers of Benjamin, played an important part in America's button needs during the 1840s.

"We look at thousands of buttons for each spring and fall season for our La Mode, Le Chic, and La Petite lines, and from those we narrow the number down substantially and then begin choosing sizes and colors," says Becky Stevens, fashion director at Blumenthal/Lansing Co. Before decisions are made, ready-to-wear and jewelry trends are carefully studied, along with domestic and international fashion forecasts and color and style information from home-sewing pattern companies. Fiber companies influence the fabric companies, who in turn influence the button companies. "We follow these developments very carefully because the buttons have to go with the fabrics."

"Timing is everything," says Becky. "Button sizes started inching back up several years ago but it wouldn't have done any good to have the larger buttons in the stores too soon because nobody would have bought them." Becky notes that much of the sewing market is shifting away from garments and into crafts, and button products have to appeal to those sewers also. "Right now one of our best selling buttons is a 1/4-inch half-ball black button that many crafters use for doll and animal eyes."

B. Blumenthal was founded in 1877 by Benjamin Blumenthal just as the American ready-to-wear industry was getting off the ground due to the perfection of the sewing

machine. Although there was a small button industry in the United States at that time, styles were dictated by Paris and 90% of the fancy buttons used in America were imported. For a time the company manufactured freshwater pearl buttons on the banks of the Mississippi River in Muscatine, Iowa, but World War I and the rapid development of plastic led to the plant's closing in 1943.

The Lindenhurst Manufacturing Company of Lindenhurst, New York produced horn buttons for Blumenthal.

In the 1950s and 1960s the company expanded with the burgeoning home-sewing industry and acquired other button companies including Lidz Brothers and Bailey, Green & Elger. In 1986 B. Blumenthal purchased the long-established Lansing Button Company and moved its packaging and distribution to Lansing, Iowa. To keep abreast of style, size, and color changes in fashion, Blumenthal/Lansing updates its lines twice a year. "Regardless of division or line, though, a good button with a classic design just goes on and on."

BECKY STEVENS
Fashion Director
Blumenthal Lansing Company

Colleen Moore emphasized the use of buttons as costume accessories in the 1926 Hollywood production of "Twinkletoes."

■ Great Gadgets

Most mail-order companies and larger fabric and craft stores carry a wide selection of gadgets designed to increase the versatility of buttons. One of the more interesting products is a variation of the traditional safety pin that allows you to wear your favorite shank buttons on any garment and then remove them with ease before laundering. Button covers are another option for increasing the wearability of special buttons, although the pins are a better choice if you don't want to risk damaging the buttons with glue. Jewelry findings designed especially to work with buttons are another great find.

"I FOUND MY FAVORITE BUTTONS ON A BUSINESS TRIP IN NEW YORK CITY ALMOST 20 YEARS AGO. WE HAD JUST RECENTLY STARTED LARK BOOKS AND I FELT LIKE A PROUD NEW FATHER, WANTING EVERYONE TO KNOW ABOUT THIS LITTLE CRAFT-BOOK PUBLISHING COMPANY. AFTER A LONG DAY OF MEETINGS, I WAS OUT FOR A MUCH-NEEDED WALK WHEN I CAME ACROSS A SMALL SHOP THAT IMMEDIATELY TRIGGERED A SENSE OF FAMILIARITY. (THE SHOP HAD BEEN MENTIONED IN A BOOK WE'D RECENTLY PUBLISHED, AND THE BOOK'S DESCRIPTION HAD CONJURED UP INTRIGUING BUTTON IMAGES.) INSIDE THE SHOP, TENDER BUTTONS, I WAS IMMEDIATELY SURROUNDED BY THOUSANDS — MAYBE HUNDREDS OF THOUSANDS — OF BUTTONS, ALL NEATLY ORGANIZED AND ARRANGED FROM THE FLOOR TO THE CEILING.

"I WANDERED AROUND FOR A FEW MINUTES, PEEKING INTO THE OCCASIONAL BOX, BUT THE SHEER NUMBER OF BUTTONS WAS JUST TOO OVERWHELMING. FINALLY, I ASKED IF THERE WERE ANY BUTTONS WITH BIRDS. THE PROPRIETORS BROUGHT ME A BOX AND LEFT ME ALONE, LIKE LIBRARIANS WHO HAVE JUST HANDED YOU A BOOK THEY KNOW YOU WILL POUR OVER FOR HOURS. I SAT THERE FOR SOME TIME, LOST IN THE BEAUTY OF THE BUTTONS, TRYING TO PICK ONE. TYPICALLY, I COULDN'T SETTLE ON ANY ONE BUTTON, AND ENDED UP SELECTING FOUR.

"THAT EVENING I CAREFULLY LOOKED OVER EACH BUTTON. EVEN THOUGH I LOVED THEM, I COULDN'T IMAGINE HOW I'D USE OR DISPLAY THEM. THEN THE IDEA CAME TO WEAR A BUTTON ON MY LAPEL. I INSERTED THE RING

SHANK INTO MY LAPEL BUT-
TONHOLE, SECURED IT FROM
BEHIND WITH A SMALL COT-
TER PIN, AND THEN WALKED
OUT ONTO THE STREETS OF
NEW YORK WITH THIS
WONDERFUL PIECE OF ART
ON MY LAPEL, A SUBTLE
REMINDER TO THE WORLD
THAT I WAS FROM LARK
BOOKS. EVEN IF CIRCUM-
STANCES REQUIRED A JACKET
AND TIE, I HAD THE BUT-
TONS TO KEEP MY OUTFIT IN
BALANCE. NOW, ALMOST 20
YEARS LATER, I STILL WEAR
THE BUTTONS PROUDLY."

ROB PULLEYN ▪ PUBLISHER ▪ FIBERARTS MAGAZINE ▪ LARK BOOKS

■ 'Tis Tedious, 'Tis True

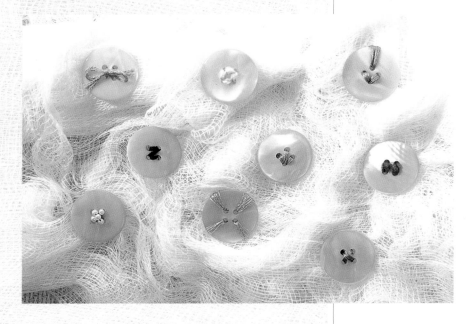

True confession time: We love playing with buttons, collecting buttons, and shopping for new buttons, but when it comes time to sew them on, most of us are less than excited. The process can be a little more interesting, though, if you're open to some changes in technique and/or materials. Consider using embroidery floss, silk crewel thread, or maybe even a metallic thread. Add a bead or two, tie some bows, invite a child to offer suggestions, but by all means, have fun.

"MY FAVORITE BUTTONS ARE ON A BRACELET THAT BELONGED TO MY HUSBAND'S FATHER'S SISTER, GENEVIEVE CLARK THOMSON. AUNT GENEVIEVE HAD COLLECTED CHARMS AND BUTTONS FROM VARIOUS PHASES OF HER LIFE AND ALWAYS WORE THEM ON THE BRACELET. THE TWO SMALLER BUTTONS ARE FROM THE COAT OF HER ONLY CHILD, A SON WHO DIED WHEN HE WAS TWO, AND GENEVIEVE ADDED THE LARGER ONE FROM MY HUSBAND'S WORLD WAR II MARINE CORPS UNIFORM. AUNT GENEVIEVE SPENT A LOT OF TIME WITH MY

DAUGHTERS WHEN THEY WERE CHILDREN AND THEY JUST ADORED HER. AUNT GENEVIEVE WAS QUITE A PERSONALITY. HER FATHER WAS SPEAKER OF THE HOUSE OF REPRESENTATIVES IN THE EARLY 1900S, AND GENEVIEVE WAS ONE OF THE FIRST WOMEN TO RUN FOR CONGRESS. THE BRACELET PASSED TO ME AFTER GENEVIEVE'S DEATH IN 1983."

MITZI CLARK

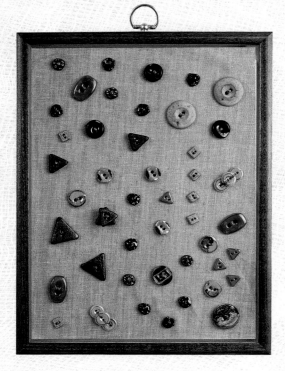

■ SHOW AND TELL

Showcasing favorite buttons has become a family business for woodcrafters Liz and Jack Shultz. The business started 12 years ago when one of Jack's coworkers brought a button case to work and asked if he could make something similar. Jack laughed at first; then he made a few cases in his workshop at night. The next year Jack and Liz took several dozen cases to a convention and they all sold. For several years afterward, Liz and Jack made cases on the weekends and at night, and they've just recently become a full-time business. "In the beginning," says Liz, "we just made a simple case and offered people the choice of stains. Today, display cases are purchased with the intent of their becoming part of the owner's interior home design, so now we offer a larger variety of colors and styles."

JACK AND LIZ SHULTZ
Shultzhaus Woodcrafters

"I SELL BEADS, BOBBLES, AND BUTTONS IN A SHOP IN NAGS HEAD, ON THE COAST OF NORTH CAROLINA, AND FOR YEARS MY CUSTOMERS HAVE BEEN BRINGING IN SPECIAL BUTTONS THEY FOUND ON THE BEACH. APPARENTLY, A SHIP THAT WAS DELIVERING A HULL FULL OF UNDRILLED MOTHER-OF-PEARL AND ABALONE BUTTONS TO BOSTON IN THE LATE 1800S TO EARLY 1900S HAD SUNK SOMEWHERE BETWEEN MILE POST 17 AND MILE POST 22, AND THE BUTTONS WERE WASHING UP. I WAS DESPERATE TO HAVE ONE OF THE BUTTONS MYSELF, BUT NO ONE WOULD TRADE OR SELL ME ONE AND ALL THE HOURS I SPENT COMBING THE BEACH WERE FRUITLESS. BUT THEN, LAST SUMMER, I LOOKED DOWN INTO A TIDE POOL AND THERE IT WAS! IT IS DEFINITELY MY FAVORITE BUTTON."

"OTHER FAVORITE BUTTONS INCLUDE THE STRING OF BUTTONS I INHERITED FROM MY GREAT GRANDMOTHER AND THREE LARGE DRAWERS OF BUTTONS I INHERITED FROM MY GRANDMOTHER. AND, IF THOSE ARE NOT ENOUGH FAVORITE BUTTONS, THERE ARE THE BUTTONS I FOUND ON THE SOUTH SIDE OF COLLINGTON HARBOR WHEN SOME FRIENDS AND I WERE CLEANING UP AN OLD DUMP SITE IN 1976."

GINNY FLOWERS ▪ CO-OWNER, CLOUD 9

"THERE ARE SOME memories that are not remembered often but that surface every now and then of really special times. When I moved from South Carolina to SoHo in 1975, one of my favorite activities was to root around Canal Street for second hand clothing, hardware, and just interesting junk in general. On one of these excursions I found a 1930's black mouton coat for $15.00. It was a beautifully styled coat and perfect for fending off the blasts of cold that tear through the winter streets of New York.

"Since my new coat needed buttons, I asked the advice of a friend, Sheryl Kagen, a bargain-savvy New Yorker who sent me off to the A. and S. Button Store on the lower East side, Essex Street off of Delancy. As I walked down to Delancy and found Essex Street, passing street vendors and the little fabric and tailoring shops in neighborhoods that hadn't changed much at all since the turn of the century, I immersed myself in the living history of the area.

"You had to walk up a dimly lit stairway to get to the shop, and it seemed amazingly small to me then. The shop had floor-to-ceiling drawers of buttons from every decade in the twentieth century and probably further back made from every possible material. I spent more time looking at buttons that I didn't need than looking at buttons for my coat. And I spent more for those four buttons than for my coat!"

DANA IRWIN ■ ART DIRECTOR

"THERE ARE SO MANY WONDERFUL BUTTONS . . . I ESPECIALLY SAVOR BUTTONS FROM VICTORIAN AND EARLIER TIMES. OVER THE YEARS WE HAVE BOUGHT A LOT OF ANTIQUE CLOTHING FOR OUR SHOP, LACIS, AND FREQUENTLY THE SELLERS BRING ALONG SEWING ROOM THINGS, WHICH FREQUENTLY INCLUDES BUTTONS. FOR A WHILE WE HAD SOME INCREDIBLE INLAID TORTOISE SHELL BUTTONS MADE AROUND THE EARLY 1700S, BUT SERIOUS BUTTON SHOPPERS, WHO USUALLY KNOW EXACTLY WHAT THEY'RE LOOKING FOR, SNAPPED THEM UP QUICKLY."

"VEGETABLE IVORY BUTTONS ARE ANOTHER FAVORITE BECAUSE OF THE HISTORY THAT GOES WITH THEM. IN THE LATE 1800S, WHEN THE USE OF IVORY WAS BANNED, VEGETABLE IVORY BUTTONS BECAME A POPULAR ALTERNATIVE AND WERE MADE THROUGH THE 1930S. OTHER BUTTONS WITH HISTORIES I FIND INTERESTING INCLUDE THE BUTTONS MADE FROM COMBINATIONS OF RUBBER AND SCRAPS DURING WORLD WAR I. THESE MOLDED BUTTONS WERE USED PRIMARILY ON MEN'S CLOTHING, ALTHOUGH THERE WERE SOME MORE INTRICATE ONES MADE FOR WOMEN'S CLOTHING."

IN THE LATE 1800S, WHEN THE USE OF IVORY WAS BANNED, VEGETABLE IVORY BUTTONS BECAME A POPULAR ALTERNATIVE AND WERE MADE THROUGH THE 1930S.

KAETHE KLIOT ■ CO-OWNER, LACIS

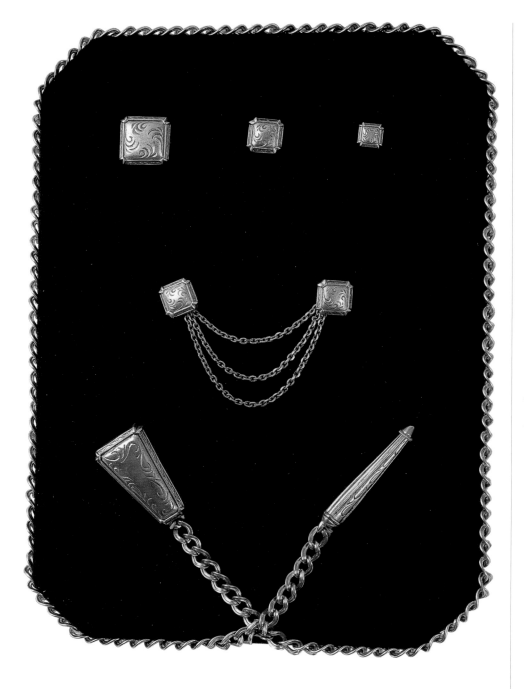

"SEVERAL TIMES A YEAR THE DESIGN TEAM AT DANA BUCHMAN DESIGNS MEETS TO FINALIZE BUTTON SELECTIONS. DANA BUCHMAN'S LINE, WHICH CATERS TO CAREER WOMEN, IS KNOWN FOR ITS ATTENTION TO DETAIL, ESPECIALLY THE BUTTONS. "ALTHOUGH THE MEETINGS TEND TO BE LOW-KEY, AN OCCASIONAL BUTTON INVOKES HEATED DEBATE, AND WHEN THE BUTTON WARRANTS IT, WE HAVE BEEN KNOWN TO ALTER THE PRICE OF A GARMENT TO AFFORD A SPECIAL BUTTON."

GIL AIMBEZ ■ DESIGNER ■ DRESS DIVISION ■ DANA BUCHMAN

■ A DAY IN THE LIFE...

"The right button looks totally effortless on a garment," says dress designer Gil Aimbez of Dana Buchman.

—————— "Buttons are an integral part of the design because they tell a customer what she can wear with the outfit (such as gold or silver jewelry), which garments she can wear over and/or under the item, whether the garment is intended for daytime or evening wear, and even the season in which the garment should be worn."

—————— When searching for buttons, Gil often visits museums and studies period jewelry for inspiration. "Although dress designs are not usually inspired by buttons, they are often inspired by an historical period, so the buttons represent the inspiration." Gil's favorite buttons tend to be simple, yet with the intricate detailing that lets you know the buttons are the work of an artist.On the more practical side, durability is a very valid part of button selections. "When we're seriously interested in a button, we run a series of stringent tests. We need to know if the button will break or discolor during drycleaning and how well it will stay on the garment when properly sewn on." Gil keeps a file book in his work area with samples of previously used buttons, along with specific details such as how well the garment sold and how durable the buttons proved through everyday wear.

—————— "For our Fall 1995 collection, buttons played an integral part in all the garments. My favorite button is from our July group, which we named 'Madrigals.' I custom-designed the buttons for this group with the goal of creating a renaissance feeling. The buttons are a beautiful, brushed antique gold with an extremely simple pattern. The button has a wonderful 1940s' shape, but it is perfect for a '90s' garment. From this button, a pocket watch look and a chain belt were also created."

Left to right: Gil Ambez, designer, dress division; Dana Buchman, designer; and Karen Harman, co-designer.

■ All in a Day's Work

"An average day at Renaissance Buttons is filled with variety," says shop manager Jan Kozma. "I might well do the advertising, sell some buttons, sweep the front stairs, show someone how to make button jewelry, look at wonderful buttons from a vendor, as well as appraise and purchase a collection. There's never a dull moment."

"We serve a variety of customers, from dry cleaners trying to replace a broken button to clothing and sweater designers who specialize in one-of-a-kind pieces and need really special buttons. Another typical customer is someone with a blazer that needs an update. They can choose from a detailed Victorian-inspired glass design to a contemporary corded fabric or carved horn. The possibilities are endless, and the customer leaves with a fresh, personalized impression of their old blazer."

"Appraising buttons is some of the more interesting work, although most people are surprised at how long the process takes. It often takes several hours to half a day just to appraise a small collection; for larger collections, we can spend the whole day and still not get through all of the buttons." Another fun part of Jan's job is working with a mail-order customer, someone several hundred (or several thousand) miles away who is looking for truly special buttons. "It's amazing how well we can work through the mail. The customer provides a fabric swatch and size, then we send them photocopies of the possibilities. After the customer has narrowed down her choices, we send the actual buttons. We rarely get returns."

Sarah McGovern, Renaissance Buttons' owner, began collecting and purchasing antique jewelry in London flea markets many years ago. Often, the jewelry she purchased came with vintage buttons, and she soon noticed that her friends were entranced with them. Sarah began selling carved bone and brass buttons wholesale in London, and then opened Renaissance Buttons in Chicago when she moved to America.

The shop is located in the Lincoln Park area, and the buttons fit in well with the 1880s' - 1890s' neighborhood architecture. About half of the shop's business comes from passersby, people who stop in for a missing button and become instantly overwhelmed by wall-to-wall buttons. Three walls are completely covered with buttons, and the fourth wall is windows. "One of the store's biggest attractions," explains Jan, "is a big steamer truck filled with ten-cent buttons. We call it the Treasure Chest. Most kids go straight for it — sometimes they even sit in it! — and the buttons make a good baby-sitter while mom shops."

"FOR ME, THE EXCITEMENT REGARDING BUTTONS HAS TO DO WITH THE RICHNESS ACHIEVED BY PLACING SO MANY LITTLE BUTTONS ONE NEXT TO THE OTHER. THE END RESULT IS SO SIMPLE, YET SO DELICATE! IN OTHER WORDS, IT IS ABOUT MANY BUTTONS, NOT ONE FAVORITE ONE. THE PHOTOGRAPH SHOWS A NATIVE CHINCHEROS INDIAN, FROM CUZCO, PERU, IN A BUTTON-EMBELLISHED GARMENT. THESE GARMENTS ARE WORN ON MARKET AND FESTIVAL DAYS, WITH MANY OF THE WOMEN PARTICIPATING IN CONTESTS TO SEE WHO CAN GET THE MOST BRAIDS

THESE GARMENTS ARE WORN ON MARKET AND FESTIVAL DAYS, WITH MANY OF THE WOMEN PARTICIPATING IN CONTESTS TO SEE WHO CAN GET THE MOST BRAIDS IN THEIR HAIR.

IN THEIR HAIR. THE BUTTON GARMENTS ARE MUCH MORE CELEBRATIONAL THAN THEIR DAY-TO-DAY CLOTHING."

ROWEN SCHUSSHEIM-ANDERSON ■ ASSOCIATE PROFESSOR, AUGUSTANA COLLEGE

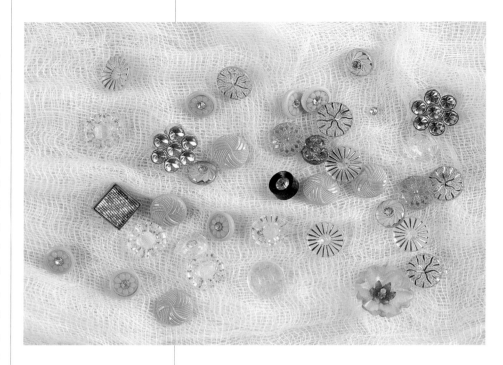

"My mother, father, younger sister, and I lived with my mother's parents until I was seven years old. Some of my earliest memories are of being nudged downstairs to visit with my grandmother, who would almost immediately set me to work at some sort of domestic play. Grandma would pull her sewing box down from the top of the refrigerator. It was an old black, metal cookie tin that never seemed to lose its oily metallic cookie smell. The bottom of the box was filled with all sorts of buttons from years of cutting buttons off of old shirts and blouses.

"I would sit down on the itchy wool floral carpet in the front parlor and sort those buttons for what seemed like hours. I'd sort them into piles of color, size, and matching shapes and in time I would always dig out the few rhinestone treasures that excited me so. They were diamonds for sure, I thought! I don't have that original box but I do have the bigger one that took its place. These buttons are a collection of the "diamonds" I have discovered through my years of hunting for diamond treasures."

"CHOOSING A FAVORITE BUTTON FROM THE 3,000-PLUS EXAMPLES IN THE COLLECTIONS OF COOPER-HEWITT, NATIONAL DESIGN MUSEUM IS PRETTY IMPOSSIBLE, BUT ONE OF MINE WOULD HAVE TO BE THE 19TH-CENTURY CARVED CAMEO BUTTON WITH THE HEAD OF DIANA. BUTTONS ARE LIKE LITTLE WINDOWS INTO THE WORLD OF DESIGN, AND THIS ONE REVEALS QUITE A BIT THROUGH ITS APPEALING IMAGERY AND UNUSUAL MATERIAL. DIANA WAS THE ANCIENT ROMAN GODDESS OF THE HUNT, THE MOON, AND CHILDBIRTH, AND SHE IS SHOWN HERE WITH HER QUIVER OF ARROWS AND CRESCENT MOON DIADEM. CLASSICAL GREEK AND ROMAN ORNAMENTAL MOTIFS WERE ESPECIALLY POPULAR DURING THE 19TH CENTURY, WHEN THE TASTE FOR HISTORICAL AND ARCHEOLOGICAL STYLES PRE-VAILED IN MANY AREAS OF THE ARTS. CAMEOS LIKE THIS ONE WERE CARVED FROM LAVA THAT WAS SAID TO HAVE BEEN LEFT BY THE ERUPTION OF MT. VESUVIUS IN THE FIRST CENTURY A.D. LAVA JEWELRY AND BUTTONS WERE POPULAR SOUVENIRS FOR 19TH-CENTURY TRAVEL-ERS TO ITALY WHO WANTED TO BRING A LITTLE OF THE ROMANCE OF ANCIENT TIMES BACK HOME WITH THEM. THIS BUTTON WAS DONATED TO THE COLLEC-TIONS BY SARAH COOPER HEWITT, WHO FOUNDED THE MUSEUM WITH HER SIS-TERS IN 1897.

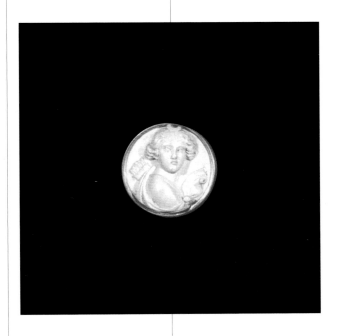

"AS A CURATOR FOR THE SMITHSONIAN INSTITUTIONS'S NATIONAL MUSEUM OF DESIGN, MY RESPONSIBILITIES INCLUDE COLLECTING, RESEARCHING, PRESERVING, ORGANIZING EXHIBITIONS, AND TEACH-ING. THE MUSEUM IS HOME TO MORE THAN A QUARTER OF A MILLION PIECES RELAT-ING TO DESIGN, ARCHITEC-TURE, AND DECORATIVE ARTS. PORTIONS OF THE BUTTON COLLECTION ARE DISPLAYED ON ROTATING SCHEDULES, AND VISITORS CAN CONTACT THE MUSEUM FOR FURTHER INFORMATION. RESEARCHERS ARE GRANTED PERMISSION WHEN POSSIBLE TO VIEW THE FULL BUTTON COLLECTION BY APPOINTMENT."

DEBORAH SAMPSON SHINN ■ ASSISTANT CURATOR OF APPLIED ARTS AND INDUSTRIAL DESIGN
COOPER-HEWITT, NATIONAL DESIGN MUSEUM, SMITHSONIAN INSTITUTION

HANDCRAFTED BUTTONS

If they haven't fallen off or come unbuttoned, most people take buttons for granted. Buttons spend their days in relative obscurity, another one of life's details that tend to get overlooked. For button crafters, though, buttons are a wonderful opportunity to play with colors, materials, and interesting shapes. Virtually every media, from woodworking to needlecrafting, can be adapted on a smaller scale to make buttons. And if you're short on time or inspiration, don't hesitate to transform an interesting found object or collectible — an old coin, a soda cap bottle, or anything else that suits your fancy — into a unique button by gluing on a shank piece or button cover.

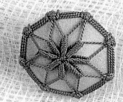

GEMSTONE BUTTONS

"You never know what you're going to find when you cut into a rock," says button maker Jim Norris, "and I just marvel at being the first human to see something made millions of years ago." These buttons are from Oregon Button Works, a part-time business begun in hopes of combining Jim's passion for lapidary with his wife Betsy's love of sewing.

I just marvel at being the first human to see something made millions of years ago."

To make the buttons, Jim cuts chunks of rocks into thin slabs. He traces individual button shapes onto the slabs, cuts the shapes out with a trim saw, and roughly smooths their edges with a grinding saw. Next, he drills the holes — the most labor-consuming part of the process. Last, the buttons go through a polishing tumbler. The buttons shown here include crazy lace agate and poppy jasper from Mexico, rhodonite from California, Turritella agate from Wyoming, picture jasper from Oregon, blue lace agate from South Africa, Brazilian agate, and sodalite.

TURK'S HEAD
KNOTTED BUTTONS

"To the beginner, the Turk's head knot looks quite complicated," says button designer Nancy Nehring. "The Turk's head knot makes an excellent ball button, or it can be combined with a second Turk's head knot opened flat to form a frog." Turk's head knots traditionally have been used on ethnic costumes as both frogs and

buttons, particularly by Eastern Europeans and the Chinese. While Nancy prefers to work her knots with leather,

designer Peg Morris creates the same button with embroidered strips of fabric and yarn. (To prepare the fabric, cut a 54" length of fabric to 3/4" wide. Press each long edge over 1/8", then press the folded edges in toward the center and secure with a decorative running stitch.)

To form the button, make an over-hand knot in one end of fabric or leather length, leaving a 1" tail on the short end. This loop will become the button

shank, and should be just large enough to fit over a pencil. Hold the overhand knot between your thumb and first finger and study the assembly diagram. (The knot is at the start position and should be held toward the back of the work, using the long tail length of leather or fabric to form the outer round of the Turk's head knot.)

Form the loops in order as labeled on the diagram. When you get to loop 3, weave the long tail over the first side of loop 2 and under the first side of loop 1. Loop 4 requires the most weaving. Pass the lacing over the second side of loop 2, under the second side of loop 1, over the first side of loop 3 and, finally, under the first side of loop 2. Pass the lacing under the first

side of loop 2 to form loop 4. Now work a second round of loops just inside the first round following the light round on the diagram.

Tighten the knot into a button and tuck the short tail up through the middle hole of the Turk's head knot. Beginning at the start position, pull up the loops in order, taking care not to tighten the overhand knot. The outer edge of the loops (at the numbers) should fall behind/below the woven central pattern and should cup around the overhand knot, leaving just enough of the

LOOP OF THE OVERHAND KNOT EXPOSED FOR A SHANK. TIGHTEN THE LOOPS A SEC-OND TIME, PULLING AS TIGHT AS POSSIBLE. CUT THE LONG TAIL OFF CLOSE TO THE SHANK ON THE BACK, THEN CUT OFF THE SHORT TAIL EVEN WITH THE TOP OF THE BUTTON. FOR A BALL-SHAPED BUTTON, ROLL THE BUTTON ON A FLAT SURFACE UNDER

overhang knot

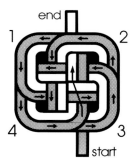

THE PALM OF YOUR HAND; FOR A FLATTER BUTTON, PRESS THE BUTTON IN A VISE. NOTE: THE LEATHER BUTTON CAN BE DIPPED IN AN ACRYLIC LEATHER FINISH IF DESIRED; REMOVE THE BUT-TON BEFORE LAUNDERING.

CROSS-STITCH BUTTONS

FOR BUTTON DESIGNER DOT ROSENSTENGEL, WHO FREQUENTLY WORKS ON LARGE, DETAILED CROSS-STITCH PROJECTS, "CROSS-STITCHING BUTTONS IS GREAT FUN BECAUSE THEY CAN BE FINISHED SO FAST." AS SHE WORKED, DOT ENVI-SIONED ROWS OF BUTTONS WITH DIFFERENT PATTERNS. "THE CHALLENGE," DOT SAYS, "WAS FINDING DESIGNS THAT CAN FIT IN SUCH A SMALL AREA." DOT ADJUSTS HER THREAD COUNTS AND THE SIZE OF HER CROSS-STITCH FABRIC TO SUIT THE DETAIL IN THE DESIGN AND THE SIZE OF THE BUTTON.

NOTE: GOLD TWIST BRAID CAN BE HOT-GLUED AROUND THE OUTSIDE EDGE OF THE BUTTON IF DESIRED. BUTTON DESIGNER: NANCY NEHRING.

THE CRAFTED DETAIL IN THESE POLYMER CLAY BUTTON COVERS REVEALS DESIGNER DOLLY LUTZ MORRIS' SKILL AT FACE MAKING. "IT'S REALLY JUST A QUESTION OF PRACTICE AND EXPERIENCE," SAYS DOLLY, A PROFESSIONAL DOLLMAKER AND SCULPTRESS WHO FREQUENTLY TEACHES CLASSES. "MANY BEGINNERS HAVE TROUBLE TRANSLATING WHAT THEIR EYES ARE SEEING INTO WHAT THEY ARE ACTUALLY DOING. IF YOU'RE MAKING A CORNUCOPIA, FOR EXAMPLE, YOU NEED TO THINK OF THE SEGMENTS SEPARATELY. A BASKET IS SIMPLY A TRIANGLE OF CLAY THAT'S BEEN CURLED UP ON ONE SIDE."

TO MAKE A CLAY BUTTON COVER, FIRST FORM A 1 TO 1-3/4" OVAL, SQUARE, HEART, OR RECTANGULAR BASE OF WHITE CLAY OVER THE BUTTON COVER. BAKE ACCORDING TO THE MANUFACTURER'S INSTRUC-

TIONS. WHEN THE CLAY HAS COOLED, BEGIN ASSEMBLING A DESIGN BY PRESSING CLAY SHAPES AGAINST THE BASE. BAKE THE BUTTON AS DIRECTED, THEN PAINT AND FINISH WITH A COAT OF CLEAR ACRYLIC

SPRAY WHEN THE PAINT HAS COMPLETELY DRIED.

DOLLY RECOMMENDS USING ORDINARY HOUSEHOLD ITEMS — TOOTHPICKS, SKEWERS, SEWING NEEDLES — TO HELP

SHAPE THE CLAY AND ADD TEXTURED DETAIL. TO CREATE A WASHED EFFECT ON HER PIECES, SHE MIXES ACRYLIC PAINTS HALF-AND-HALF WITH A CONTROL MEDIUM. "BEGINNERS ARE OFTEN DISAPPOINTED WITH THEIR PAINTING RESULTS, BUT IT TAKES A VERY FINE POINT BRUSH AND SOME PRACTICE FOR GOOD RESULTS." A COAT OF ANTIQUING MEDIUM THINNED WITH A CONTROL MEDIUM ADDED AFTER THE FIRST COAT OF PAINT DRIES CAN HELP BRING OUT DEPTH IN A PIECE.

TWILL BUTTONS

DESIGNER KIMBERLY SHUCK LOVES COMPLEX RIVERCANE TWILL BASKETRY PATTERNS AND HAS ADAPTED THEM FOR USE IN THESE WHITE-ASH SPLINT BUTTONS. "WHAT I LIKE MOST ABOUT THE BUTTONS IS THAT THEY ARE SO SUBTLE. THEY ARE ALMOST PRIVATE BECAUSE MOST PEOPLE NEVER LOOK CLOSELY ENOUGH TO SEE THE PATTERN."

TO MAKE A LARGE TWILL BUTTON, CUT 1/16"-WIDE ASH SPLINT INTO 3" STRIPS AND SOAK THEM TO MAKE THEM MORE FLEXIBLE. BROWSE THROUGH SOME TWILL PATTERN BOOKS AND GRAPH ONE THAT YOU LIKE. LAY OUT ALL THE VERTICAL STRIPS AND THEN WEAVE IN THE HORIZONAL STRIPS, USING A HEAVY BOOK TO HOLD ONE EDGE OF THE STRIPS IN PLACE.

"ONCE THE SPLINT HAS BEEN WOVEN," SAYS KIMBERLY, "IT CAN BE TREATED AS A RATHER UNCOOPER-ATIVE PIECE OF FABRIC AND ASSEMBLED INTO A BUTTON WITH A BUTTON-COVERING KIT." DAMPEN THE WOVEN FABRIC AND CENTER IT IN THE RUBBER SHAPE FORMER. PLACE THE METAL PIECE OVER THE SHAPE FORMER ACCORDING TO THE MANU-FACTURER'S INSTRUCTIONS AND TRIM THE EXCESS SPLINT. KIMBERLY WARNS BUTTON CRAFTERS THAT THESE BUTTONS ARE VERY HARD TO SEAL. "EXERCISE GREAT PATIENCE AND GREAT PRESSURE. GOOD LUCK, AND DON'T FORGET TO BREATHE."

"I SAW MY FIRST ANTIQUE Victorian crocheted button at Lacis in California," says button designer Nancy Nehring, "and I went home determined to reproduce one." A lace expert told Nancy that written instructions for the technique apparently didn't exist, but

took the time to explain how to make the long, spiral bullion stitch. (The bullion is nearly a lost stitch.) "I spent more than two hours making my first bullion stitch and more than two years perfecting my crochet technique."

For the blue button (Four Fans) you will need a #12 crochet hook, some #12 pearl cotton, a #60 button mold covered with fabric, and a 1/4" PET ring. In round 1, attach the thread to the ring; chain 2; (yarn over 10 bullion, single crochet) 6 times; slipstitch to join. In round 2, chain 2; (2 yarn over 10 bullion in top of bullion of previous round, chain 5) around. In round 3, slipstitch between bullion; chain 1; (chain 1, 2 yarn over 10 bullion between bullion pair of previous round, chain 1, 8 single crochet over chain 5) around; slipstitch to join. In round 4, slipstitch between the bullion; chain 1; (chain 1, 1 yarn over 10 bullion between bullion pair of previous round, chain 1, single crochet in each

single crochet of previous round) around; slipstitch to join. In round 5, single crochet in every stitch of previous round for 4 rounds. In round 6, insert the mold; single crochet in every other stitch of the

"I SPENT MORE THAN TWO HOURS MAKING MY FIRST BULLION STITCH AND MORE THAN TWO YEARS PERFECTING MY CROCHET TECHNIQUE."

previous round for 2 rounds; tie off.

For the pink button (Stacked Bullion) you will need a #12 crochet hook, some #12 pearl cotton, a #60 button mold covered with fabric, a 1/4" PET ring,

bullion stitch

PET ring

finish with slip stitch

BRASS RING. FOR ROUND 1, ATTACH THE THREAD TO THE RING; CHAIN 1; (YARN OVER 10 BULLION, SINGLE CROCHET OVER RING) 8 TIMES; SLIP-STITCH TO JOIN. IN ROUND 2, DROP HOOK; PLACE CROCHET CENTER INSIDE BRASS RING WITH THREAD TO BACK OF RING AND LOOP TO FRONT; PICK UP LOOP; (SINGLE CRO-CHET IN TOP OF BULLION, 6 SINGLE CROCHET OVER RING) AROUND; JOIN. IN ROUND 3, CHAIN 3, SINGLE CROCHET IN NEXT SPACE; (CHAIN 8, SKIP 1 BULLION, SINGLE CRO-CHET ABOVE NEXT BULLION, CHAIN 2, SINGLE CROCHET IN NEXT STITCH) AROUND. IN ROUND 4, (4 YARN OVER 8 BULLIONS OVER CHAIN 2, 15 SINGLE CROCHETS OVER CHAIN 8) AROUND. IN ROUND 5, SINGLE CROCHET IN EACH STITCH OF PREVIOUS ROUND FOR 7 ROUNDS. IN ROUND 6, INSERT THE MOLD; SINGLE CROCHET IN EVERY OTHER STITCH FOR 2 ROUNDS; TIE OFF.

GLASS-BEAD MAKER KIMBERLEY ADAMS SAW GLASS BUTTONS AS A NATUR-AL EXTENSION OF HER WORK WITH BEADS. "I DO A LOT OF SEWING AND HAVE DONE SOME FASHION DESIGN, SO GLASS BUTTONS WERE AN

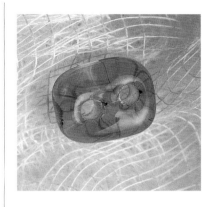

THIS CASE, SEWING HOLES.) KIM USES AN ASSORTMENT OF SMALL PLIERS AND TWEEZERS TO HELP PULL AND TWIST THE GLASS UNTIL SHE'S HAPPY WITH THE SHAPE AND TEXTURE OF THE BUTTONS.

INTRIGUING IDEA. THE ONLY CHALLENGE," SAYS KIM, "WAS IN FINDING A WAY TO HOLD TWO MAN-DRELS STEADY WHILE WORK-ING THE LIQUID GLASS AROUND THEM." (A MAN-DREL IS THE METAL WIRE THAT LIQUID GLASS IS FORMED AROUND; AFTER THE GLASS COOLS, IT IS REMOVED, LEAVING A THREADING HOLE, OR IN

NEEDLE LACE BUTTONS

"Needle lace buttons seem to be one of the few Victorian crafts that have not enjoyed a revival in public interest," explains button designer Nancy Nehring. Researching the history of these buttons made them come alive for Nancy. Handmade buttons were used before 1850 and primarily were made by women and children lacemakers on a piece-work basis for low pay in poor working conditions to support the Paris fashion industry. The Franco-Prussian war, increasing industrialization, and World War I's wide use of plastics all contributed to undercutting prices and putting lace button makers out of business.

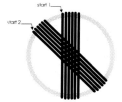

"Some button designers make buttons for show and do not consider the buyer who may wish to use the button on a garment. For the most part, my buttons are specifically designed to be functional, and I enjoy creating them for a wide range of customers, including fashion designers, historical costumers, collectors, brides, wearable-arts people, and seamstresses."

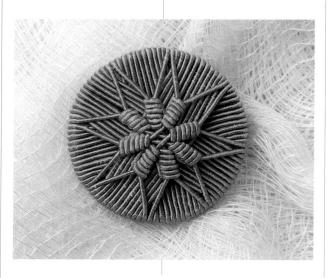

HANDMADE BUTTONS WERE USED BEFORE 1850 AND PRIMARILY WERE MADE BY WOMEN AND CHILDREN LACEMAKERS ON A PIECE-WORK BASIS FOR LOW PAY IN POOR WORKING CONDITIONS TO SUPPORT THE PARIS FASHION INDUSTRY.

To make a Morning Star button (the blue button) you will need a 1" flat wood mold, 2-1/2 yards of #3 gimp, a pair of small scissors, and a #20 tapestry needle. Hold one end of the gimp at the center back of the button; wrap the gimp around the button 7 times, making the first wrap to the left and working to the right. Rotate the button 45 degrees clockwise; then make 7 more wraps with the first wrap to the left and working to the right. Rotate and repeat the wrapping two more times.

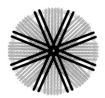

Starting with the gimp at the back, wrap the gimp across the front of the button twice in each gap between the previous groups. Thread the gimp onto a tapestry needle. Pass the needle from the back through the hole in the center of the mold to the front. Take one strand of gimp from each of two adjacent wraps and overcast them together 4 times each. Work from the center out, as near to the center of the button as possible.

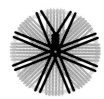

Move back to the center of the button with the gimp lying to the side of the 4 over-

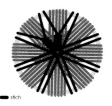

CAST STITCHES. OVERCAST THE LONE STRAND OF GIMP FROM ONE OF THE TWO PREVIOUS PAIRS AND ONE STRAND FROM AN ADJACENT NEW PAIR. CONTINUE AROUND THE BUTTON UNTIL ALL PAIRS ARE WRAPPED. PASS THE NEEDLE AND GIMP THROUGH THE HOLE IN THE MOLD TO THE BACK AND TIE OFF. (CARE NOTE: REMOVE BUTTONS BEFORE WASHING IF POSSIBLE; BUTTONS CAN BE HAND WASHED; DRY WITH A HAIR DRYER.)

To make an EVENING STAR button (THE PURPLE BUTTON) YOU WILL NEED A 7/8" DOMED WOOD MOLD, 3 YARDS OF #3 GIMP, A #20 TAPESTRY NEEDLE, A #8 EMBROIDERY NEEDLE, A PAIR OF SMALL SCISSORS, AND QUILTING THREAD. HOLD ONE END OF THE GIMP AT THE CENTER BACK OF THE BUTTON. WRAP THE GIMP AROUND THE BUTTON 4 TIMES, MAKING THE FIRST WRAP TO THE LEFT AND WORKING TO THE RIGHT.

ROTATE THE BUTTON 45 DEGREES CLOCKWISE, THEN MAKE 4 MORE WRAPS WITH THE FIRST WRAP TO THE LEFT, WORKING TO THE RIGHT. ROTATE AND REPEAT WRAPPING TWO MORE TIMES.

STARTING WITH THE GIMP AT THE BACK, WRAP THE GIMP ACROSS THE FRONT OF THE BUTTON ONCE TO THE LEFT OF A GROUP OF 4 WRAPS. TURN THE BUTTON CLOCKWISE AND WRAP TO THE LEFT OF THE NEXT GROUP OF 4. CONTINUE AROUND THE BUTTON FOR 3 ROUNDS. THREAD THE GIMP ONTO THE TAPESTRY NEEDLE. ON THE BACK, PASS THE NEEDLE AND GIMP UNDER THE PREVIOUS WRAPS NEAR THE CENTER TO KEEP THE PREVIOUS WRAPS FROM SLIPPING OFF THE MOLD. TIE OFF.

THREAD THE QUILTING THREAD INTO THE EMBROIDERY NEEDLE. STITCH 2 STRANDS OF GIMP IN PLACE WHERE THE LAST ROUND OF WRAPS FORMS A POINT. THESE POINT-FORMING STRANDS SHOULD CROSS EACH OTHER. RUN THE NEEDLE AND THREAD UNDER 8 STRANDS OF GIMP ON TOP OF THE BUTTON TO THE NEXT POINT. STITCH 2 STRANDS OF GIMP TOGETHER TO FORM A POINT. CONTINUE AROUND THE BUTTON, THEN TIE THE THREAD OFF ON THE BACK SIDE. (CARE NOTE: REMOVE THE BUTTONS FROM THE GARMENT BEFORE WASHING IF POSSIBLE; BUTTONS ARE HAND WASHABLE; DRY WITH A HAIR DRYER.)

To make a SHIRTWAIST button (THE GREEN AND IVORY BUTTON) YOU WILL NEED A 9/16" BRASS RING, 3-1/2 YARDS OF #30 COTTON CROCHET THREAD, AND A #24 TAPESTRY NEEDLE. TIE ONE END OF THE CROCHET THREAD ONTO THE RING. WRAP THE THREAD AROUND THE RING TIGHTLY, CROSSING THE CENTER AND EVENLY SPACING THE WRAPS AROUND THE RING 15 TIMES AND ENDING AT THE CENTER BACK TO GIVE 30 SPOKES.

COUNTING THE 30TH SPOKE AS SPOKE #1, COUNT CLOCKWISE 10 SPOKES (1/3 THE NUMBER OF SPOKES, SPOKE #17 ON THE FIRST ILLUSTRATION) AND LOOSELY WRAP THE THREAD FROM THE BACK TO THE FRONT ON THE FAR SIDE NEXT TO THIS SPOKE (REFER TO THE SECOND ILLUSTRATION), USING SPOKE #17 AS

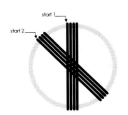

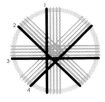

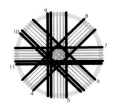

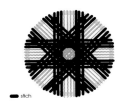

AN ANCHOR. ON THE FRONT OF THE BUTTON, WRAP THE THREAD NEXT TO SPOKE 28 (ILLUSTRATION 2B) AS AN ANCHOR. IF YOU HAVE TROUBLE GETTING THE SPOKES TO HOLD, MOVE DOWN 1 OR 2 MORE SPOKES (1/3 PLUS 1 OR 1/3 PLUS 2) AND/OR LIGHTLY SAND THE OUTER EDGE OF THE RING WITH 320-GRIT SANDPAPER.

ON THE BACK, WRAP THE THREAD TO SPOKE 15 (ILLUSTRATION 3C) AND THEN ON THE FRONT TO SPOKE 26 (ILLUSTRATION 3D). CONTINUE AROUND THE RING. WHEN YOU GET TO "U" (ILLUSTRATION 4) THE THREAD WRAPS ON THE OTHER SIDE OF SPOKE 28 FROM WHERE "B" WRAPPED. EACH OF THE 30 SPOKES WILL NOW HAVE 1 NEW WRAP ON EACH SIDE OF IT, MAKING 30 SETS OF 3 STRANDS EACH.

CUT OFF ABOUT 3 FEET OF THREAD AND THREAD IT IN THE NEEDLE. COME UP FROM THE BACK TO THE FRONT NEAR THE

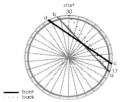
front
back

CENTER OF THE RING. OVERCAST BETWEEN EACH SET OF 3 THREADS (ILLUSTRATION 5), CATCHING ONLY THE TOP LAYER OF THREADS. TO FORM THE WINDOW, RUN THE NEEDLE FROM THE OUTSIDE TOWARD THE CENTER UNDER THE THREADS, THEN BACK OVER THE TOP OF THE THREADS TO THE NEXT SET.

ADD BUTTONHOLE STITCHES OVER THE RING BETWEEN EACH SET OF 3 THREADS. USE 1, 2, OR MORE DEPENDING ON THE NUMBER NEEDED TO COVER THE RING. KEEP THE BAR OF THE BUTTONHOLE STITCH TO THE BACK OF THE BUTTON. TIE OFF THE THREAD AT THE CENTER. (CARE NOTE:

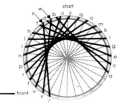
front

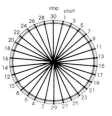

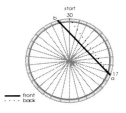
front
back

MACHINE WASHABLE AND DRYABLE.)

TO MAKE THE VICTORIAN STAR BUTTON (THE BROWN BUTTON) YOU WILL NEED A 3/4" WOOD MOLD, A 3" SQUARE OF LINING FABRIC; A LENGTH OF #4 SILK BEAD CORD, QUILTING THREAD, A #7 EMBROIDERY NEEDLE, A NEEDLE GRABBER OR NEEDLE NOSED PLIERS, AND A #26 TAPESTRY NEEDLE.

CUT A 2-1/8" CIRCLE FROM THE LINING FABRIC AND MAKE RUNNING STITCHES 1/4" IN FROM THE EDGES. INSERT THE BEAD INTO THE CENTER WITH THE FLAT SIDE TOWARD THE OPENING AND DRAW THE

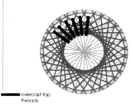
overcast top threads

THREAD UPRIGHT TO GATHER IT AROUND THE BEAD. SEW THE OPENING SHUT. IF THE FABRIC IS NOT STRETCHED TIGHT OVER THE MOLD, WORK A HERRINGBONE STITCH IN A CLOCKWISE PATTERN.

TO WORK A HERRINGBONE STITCH, TAKE A STITCH IN THE FABRIC HALFWAY BETWEEN THE CENTER AND OUTSIDE EDGE. CROSS BACK AND TAKE A STITCH, CATCHING THE FABRIC ABOUT HALFWAY BETWEEN THE CENTER AND OUTSIDE EDGE ON THE OPPOSITE SIDE. CROSS BACK TO THE FIRST SIDE, ROTATE THE BUTTON SLIGHTLY TO THE NEXT GATHER, AND TAKE ANOTHER STITCH. CONTINUE ALTERNATING SIDES AND STITCHES AROUND THE BUTTON BACK AND TIE OFF.

UNWIND THE SILK CORD AND CUT OFF THE WIRE NEEDLE. THREAD ABOUT 2" INTO THE EMBROIDERY NEEDLE. (YOU MAY NEED A NEEDLETHREADER

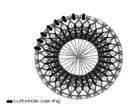
buttonhole over ring

AND WILL HAVE TO FLATTEN THE END OF THE CORD TO GET IT THROUGH THE EYE.) TAKE 2 SMALL STITCHES THROUGH THE LINING NEAR THE CENTER BACK, LEAVING A 1" LENGTH TO ANCHOR THE CORD.

WRAP THE BUTTON IN THE 12 TO 6 O'CLOCK PATTERN SHOWN IN THE ILLUSTRATION SO THAT THE CORD CROSSES THE TOP OF THE BUTTON TWICE IN EACH OF 4 POSITIONS, MAKING 8 BARS FOR WEAVING. TO ANCHOR THE BARS ON THE FRONT, COME UP TO THE FRONT FROM THE BACK THROUGH THE CENTER HOLE AND CROSS OVER THE CORDS WHERE THEY MEET IN THE CENTER, THEN GO DOWN TO THE BACK. KNOT THE CORDS TOGETHER ON THE BACK WHERE THE CORDS CROSS BUT DO NOT CUT. ADJUST THE BARS ON THE FRONT SO THEY ARE EVENLY SPACED AND CROSS AT THE CENTER.

TO WEAVE THE CENTER PATTERN, BRING THE CORD BACK UP THROUGH THE CENTER HOLE TO THE FRONT. OVERCAST AROUND 1 CORD FROM EACH OF 2 ADJACENT BARS 10 TIMES FROM THE CENTER OUT. MOVE BACK TO THE CENTER OF THE BUTTON. THE SILK CORD SHOULD BE LYING TO ONE SIDE OF THE 10 OVERCAST STITCHES YOU HAVE JUST MADE. USE THE LONE BAR AND ONE BAR FROM THE NEXT PAIR OF BARS AND OVERCAST OVER THESE TWO 10 TIMES. CONTINUE AROUND THE BUTTON UNTIL ALL 8 PAIRS HAVE BEEN OVERCASTED TOGETHER.

THE OUTER EDGE PATTERN IS 3 ROUNDS OF BACKSTITCH. MOVE TO THE OUTER EDGE BY LAYING THE SILK CORD ALONG 1 BAR OF THE LAST PAIR OVERCAST. WORK A BACKSTITCH OVER 2 ADJACENT BARS SO THAT THE CORD BETWEEN THE BARS IS ON TOP OF THE BARS. CONTINUE AROUND THE BUTTON 3 TIMES.

RUN THE NEEDLE THROUGH THE LINING ABOUT 1/3 OF THE WAY TO THE CENTER ON THE BUTTON BACK TO HOLD THE BACKSTITCHES IN PLACE. ON THE BUTTON FRONT, GO UNDER THE BARS BETWEEN THE 3 BACKSTITCHES AND THE CENTER OF THE BUTTON. STITCH UNDER THE LINING ON THE BACK TO HOLD THE CORD IN PLACE. REPEAT ON THE NEXT SECTIONS. TIE THE CORD AT THE CENTER BUT DO NOT CUT.

ADD A SHANK TO THE BUTTON IF DESIRED BY STITCHING 2 ROUNDS OF A RECTANGLE WITH THE SHORT SIDES UNDER THE LINING AND THE LONG SIDES ON TOP OF THE LINING ON THE CENTER BACK. WEAVE OVER THE LONG SIDES OF THE RECTANGLE BY PASSING THE CORD DOWN AT THE CENTER BETWEEN THE 2 SIDES OF THE RECTANGLE, UP OVER THE OUTER EDGE, AND BACK DOWN AT THE CENTER. ALTERNATE ON OPPOSITE SIDES OF THE RECTANGLE. TIE OFF AND CUT THE CORD. (CARE NOTE: DRY CLEAN THE GARMENT OR REMOVE THE BUTTONS BEFORE LAUNDERING.)

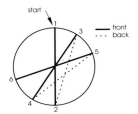

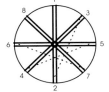

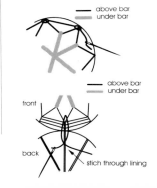

STAMP BUTTON

Textile artist Sara Long transformed canceled AIDS stamps into buttons to embellish a quilt. "The quilt, AIDS Web, is an historical piece that explores the political and social implications of AIDS." The quilt was recently juried into the biennial Quilt National exhibit.

To make a stamp button, cut out a piece of foam core slightly larger than the stamp. Glue a decorative piece of paper over the foam core, then center the stamp over the paper and glue it in place. Glue a shank finding to the center back of the foam core, then finish with a coat of clear adhesive spray. Note: To remove a canceled stamp from an envelope, float the envelope on the top of some water until the stamp loosens. Remove the stamp and place it on paper towels to dry.

Designer Ayelet Lindenstrauss works her buttons on silk gauze in an assortment of canvas embroidery techniques, and then mounts the buttons with commercial button-making kits. "I really enjoy using the silk gauze for the buttons," says Ayelet, "which is to my mind the most flexible and versatile ground for

canvas embroidery. When stitched, silk gauze gives fabric which is exactly the ideal weight for commercial button kits" (Ayelet uses a #40 mesh.) "I think the gauze is not as popular as it could be because people treat it

with too much care, assuming they have to use it with silk floss, special needles, and very rigid stitching procedures — all of which is not true!" With some of her buttons, Ayelet embroiders on the gauze and then appliques the embroidery onto a piece of fabric, or creates more three-dimensional looks by

forming distortions with the gauze during the stitching and then padding the distortion with stuffing before mounting the button. Ayelet's design inspirations often come from

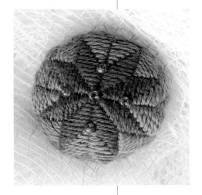

old Indian embroideries, and she enjoys embellishing the embroidery with special beads. (The smaller blue button uses porcelain tile beads from Czechoslovakia.)

CLAY FACES

"I've always been intrigued with buttons, and just being around them makes me want to grab a big handful," says clay jewelry designer Marg Kuhl. Three years ago Marg and a friend rented a studio for painting and work with clay, but the clay was so much fun that they didn't finish many paintings, and Marg now works in her home studio. "I really enjoy watching personalities emerge from the clay faces. When I'm designing, I try to keep my approach very playful and just let the clay go where it likes."

To make her buttons, Marg positions thin slices from a face cane onto a clay base and then adds collages of clay details until she's happy with the piece. She burnishes the layers together, bakes them, and then drills button holes. Marg suggests that serious beginners invest in a pasta maker, a food processor (both used to condition clay), and an illustrated how-to book to help learn the basics of making multicolor clay canes. "Don't be frugal with your clay during the learning process," Marg recommends. "The only way to develop your own style is to keep trying new techniques."

P A I N T E D   B U T T O N S

GRAPHIC DESIGNER AND PRINTMAKER SARA ATLEE HODGSON BEGAN PAINTING BUTTONS ONE CHRISTMAS WHEN SHE WAS SHORT ON GIFT-BUYING FUNDS. INSTEAD OF PURCHASING A GIFT FOR HER MOM, AN AVID BUTTON COLLECTOR, SARA DECIDED TO PAINT A CUSTOM BUTTON. "MY MOTHER REALLY LIKED THE BUTTON, AND SHE ENCOURAGED ME TO EXHIBIT THEM. THE BUTTONS WERE A BIG HIT, AND I'VE BEEN PAINTING THEM EVER SINCE." SARA'S ARTWORK IS DONE ON A SHEET OF POLYSTYRENE WHICH SHE MOLDS OVER A LACROSSE BALL TO FORM A DOMED EFFECT. IN ADDITION TO ACRYLIC PAINTS, SHE USES PRIMA COLOR PENCILS, ALL KINDS OF MARKERS, AND RAPIDIOGRAPHS. TO PROTECT THE FINISHED ART, THE SURFACE IS COVERED WITH ACRYLIC VARNISH. THE ART IS THEN MOUNTED ON A SEW-THROUGH BUTTON WITH A DISH SHAPE AND A SHANK IS ADDED.

WHEN BEAD ARTIST KIMBERLY SHUCK BEGAN COLLEGE YEARS AGO, SHE INTENDED TO BECOME A TRANSLATOR AND ENROLLED IN A TEXTILE HISTORY CLASS TO SATISFY A GENERAL EDUCATION REQUIREMENT. "I HAD A (REPORTEDLY IRRITATING) NERVOUS HABIT OF BEADING AT THAT TIME," REMEMBERS KIMBERLY, "AND I BROUGHT MY BEADWORK TO EVERY CLASS." RATHER THAN VIEWING KIMBERLY'S BEADING AS A DISTRACTION, THE PROFESSOR ENCOURAGED HER TO CONTINUE, POINTING OUT THAT BEADWORK WAS A LEGITIMATE TEXTILE TECHNIQUE. "IT OCCURRED TO ME THAT RATHER THAN WORRYING ABOUT WHAT I NEEDED TO BECOME 'WHEN I GREW UP,' I SHOULD HONOR WHAT I ALREADY WAS."

A MIXED-RACE TSALAGI INDIAN WHOSE PEOPLE ARE FROM THE GOING SNAKE AREA OF NORTHEASTERN OKLAHOMA, KIMBERLY WAS INITIALLY EXPOSED TO BEADWORK AS PART OF THE DESIGN AND CREATION OF POWWOW REGALIA. "BEING ASKED TO WORK ON SOMEONE ELSE'S REGALIA IS A GREAT HONOR. IT'S ALSO AN EXERCISE IN HUMILITY IN THAT MANY PEOPLE MAY CONTRIBUTE TO

"BEING ASKED TO WORK ON SOMEONE ELSE'S POWWOW REGALIA IS A GREAT HONOR."

THE SAME OUTFIT, MAKING THE WORK BOTH YOURS AND NOT YOURS."

KIMBERLY USES SEVERAL EMBROIDERY TECHNIQUES TO BEAD HER BUTTONS, INCLUDING THE TWO-STRAND METHOD, THE ROSETTE TECHNIQUES, AND THE PEYOTE STITCH. TO ENSURE SUCCESS FOR BEADING BUTTONS, KIMBERLY RECOMMENDS USING A COMMERCIAL BUTTON-COVERING KIT AND AN EASY-TO-BEAD-UPON FABRIC. (KIMBERLY'S FAVORITE FABRIC IS AUTOMOTIVE CHAMOIS, WHICH SHE SUNS ON BOTH SIDES BEFORE USING TO REMOVE THE OILY SMELL.) KIMBERLY STARTS BEADING ON THE OUTER EDGE AND WORKS INWARD AND LIKE MANY BEADS ARTISTS SHE IS SOMETIMES DISTRACTED BY THE NATURALLY OCCURRING SPACES BETWEEN THE ROWS OF BEADS. "I TRIED USING SMALLER BEADS, BUT THE SPACES WERE STILL THERE, JUST PROPORTIONATELY SMALLER. I FINALLY GAVE UP AND LEARNED TO LOVE THOSE SPACES." THE CORN BUTTON WAS MADE FROM A SOFT LEATHER AND INSPIRED BY SOME OF THE NEWER JAPANESE SEED BEADS THAT COME IN SEVERAL CORNLIKE COLORS.

P O R C E L A I N
B U T T O N S

"I DON'T HAVE A BUSINESS CARD," SAYS MULTIMEDIA ARTIST COLLEEN TRETTER, "SO I OFTEN GIVE OUT BUTTONS INSTEAD." (COLLEEN'S BUTTON INVENTORY IS RUNNING LOW, THOUGH, SO SHE'S RESOLVED TO BREAK THIS HABIT.) "I HAVE THIS DESIRE TO CREATE THINGS THAT ARE UNEXPECTED, AND A HANDCRAFTED BUTTON IS AN UNEXPECTED SURPRISE."

EVERY STEP IN COLLEEN'S BUTTON-MAKING PROCESS IS DONE BY HAND, FROM CUTTING, SHAPING, STAMPING, AND HOLE-PUNCHING TO

"I HAVE THIS DESIRE TO CREATE THINGS THAT ARE UNEXPECTED, AND A HANDCRAFTED BUTTON IS AN UNEXPECTED SURPRISE."

THE GLAZING, AND THE PATTERNS IN HER BUTTONS REVEAL HER LOVE OF TEXTILES. "I FIRE THE BUTTONS

IN A SALT KILN, EVEN THOUGH IT'S MORE WORK, SO THE BUTTONS WILL KEEP THEIR WONDERFUL CLANKETY SOUND."

TEMARI BALL BUTTONS

"I AM STRUCK BY THE BY THE UNIVERSALITY OF THE FIBER ARTS," SAYS KNIT DESIGNER KATHLEEN POWER JOHNSON. "BASICALLY, WE KNOT AND LOOP AND LACE. IT'S SO DELIGHTFUL TO COMBINE THESE DISCIPLINES IN NEW WAYS TO CREATE A NEW ART FORM IN FIBER ART BUTTONS." KATHLEEN USES *TEMARI* BUTTONS ON MANY OF HER SPECIALTY KNITS BECAUSE THEIR INTRICATE, JEWEL-LIKE QUALITY ADDS A UNIQUE BEAUTY.

TO MAKE A *TEMARI* BALL BUTTON YOU WILL NEED A BUTTON FORM, SELF-ADHESIVE GAUZE FOR PADDING, 3 COLORS OF METALLIC OR COTTON THREAD, AND A NEEDLE. SHAPE SEVERAL LAYERS OF PADDING MATERIAL AROUND THE BUTTON FORM, HOLD- ING THEM TOGETHER ON THE BACK SIDE. COMPLETELY COVER THE PADDING WITH RANDOM WRAPS OF SEWING THREAD. CUT THE WRAP-

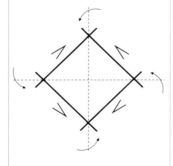

PING THREAD, LEAVING A 12" TAIL, THEN THREAD THE TAIL IN A NEEDLE AND TAKE SMALL TACKING STITCHES AROUND THE BUTTON, END- ING WITH SEVERAL OVERLAP- PING BACKSTITCHES ON THE

BACK SIDE. IF NECESSARY, REDISTRIBUTE THE THREADS WITH THE NEEDLE'S EYE.

AT THIS POINT THE BUTTON (KNOWN AS THE *MARI*) IS DIVIDED WITH MARKER THREADS INTO SEC-

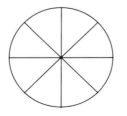

TIONS, TRADITIONALLY QUARTERS, SIXTHS, EIGHTS, OR TENTHS. THE MARKER THREADS PROVIDE A FRAME- WORK FOR THE EMBROIDERY STITCHES AND THE DESIGN; THEY CAN BE REMOVED AFTER THE DESIGN IS COM- PLETED. FOR THE WOVEN SQUARE BUTTON SHOWN HERE, DIVIDE THE BUTTON FRONT INTO EIGHTS BY FIRST TAKING SEVERAL BACK- STITCHES WITH A SHARP NEEDLE ON THE BACK SIDE OF THE BUTTON AND THEN WRAPPING THE BUTTON FOUR TIMES TO CREATE 8 SECTIONS, TAKING A STITCH ON THE BACK SIDE OF THE BUTTON EACH TIME YOU CHANGE DIRECTION WITH A LENGTH OF THREADED METALLIC OR COTTON THREAD. FASTEN OFF WITH SEVERAL BACKSTITCHES.

MOST *TEMARI* DESIGNS BEGIN AT THE CEN- TER AND WORK CIRCULARLY OUTWARD, CHANGING COLOR AS THEY DEVELOP.

For this button the traditional herringbone stitch is worked over the marker threads. To make a herringbone stitch, take small backstitches under and over the marking threads, referring to the illustration as you work and moving clockwise. Make the first square by working herringbone stitches over every other thread, starting with your needle close to the outside edge of the button and coming up about 1/4" from the center. Work 2 rounds of stitching in color #1, 1 in metallic thread and 2 rounds in color #2. Begin each new color by coming up by the thread just before your last stitch. Repeat the same color sequence on the 4 alternate marker threads (the dotted lines in the illustration), weaving over each group of 5 threads from the first square. Bury the thread end and cut it. The background thread wraps will still show around the button's edges. Traditional Japanese *temari* allows the threads to show; they can be covered with decorative herringbone or straight stitches if desired.

S Q U A W   B U T T O N

Knit designer Kathleen Power Johnson's squaw buttons combine basket-making techniques with multicolored silk and metallic threads with striking results. "I devote a tremendous amount of

time and energy designing unique knit garments which cry out for equally special buttons to complete the effect. For me, designing the buttons has become an integral part of the process."

━━━ To make a squaw button you will need a 1" plastic ring, a 3/4" plastic ring, a #22 tapestry needle, some hand-dyed plied silk embroidery thread, and some gold thread. Begin by threading several plies of the silk thread onto the needle. Hold the rings together with the smaller one inside the larger and wrap both rings together 4 times, taking care not to make the wraps too tight. Next, wrap the outside ring twice. Repeat this sequence until the ring is covered snugly, then add approximately one wrap of gold thread for each set of silk threads.

CZECHOSLOVAKIAN CERAMIC BUTTONS

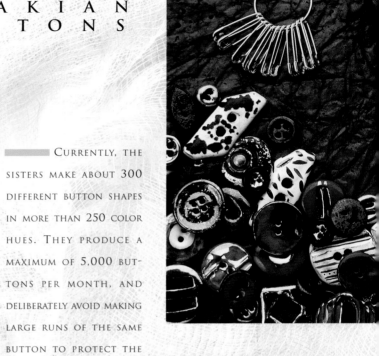

Sisters Magdalena Dyntarová and Štěpánka Denková, of Stechovice, Czechoslovakia, began making ceramic buttons in 1990 after the revolution offered Czechoslovakian citizens new enterprise projects. They live near the community of Davle, which was a major producer of buttons during the time of the first republic (1918 - 1938). "After World War II, when the communist government took over our republic and socialism began, everything that could not be manufactured on assembly lines was considered uneconomical, and handcrafted buttons stopped being produced. Our goal is to link ourselves to the old button-making tradition."

"OUR GOAL IS TO LINK OURSELVES TO THE OLD CZECH BUTTON-MAKING TRADITION."

Currently, the sisters make about 300 different button shapes in more than 250 color hues. They produce a maximum of 5,000 buttons per month, and deliberately avoid making large runs of the same button to protect the buttons' originality. All glazing and decorating is done by hand with a brush and pen, using only classic ceramic materials and colors. "The interesting thing about designing new buttons is that it's never possible to exhaust all the shape and color variations. Some day, we hope to work with a garment designer — it would be great fun to devise color and shape combinations for specific garments."

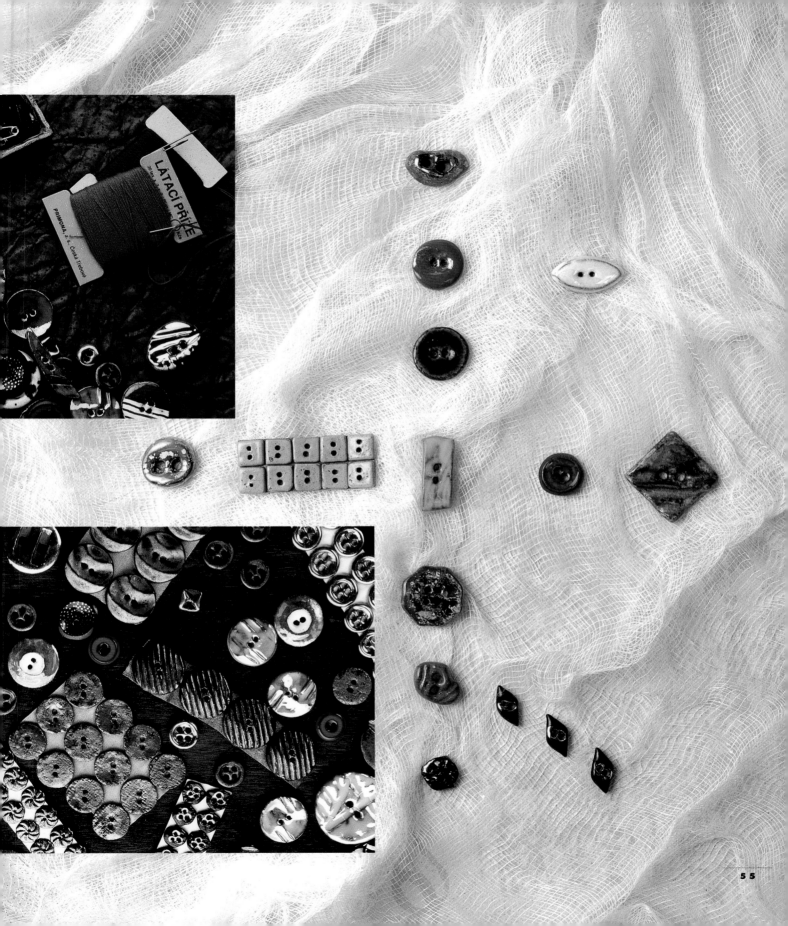

P A P E R B U T T O N S

Designer Heather
Allen encountered more
problems than she antic-
ipated when she made
these buttons. Her ini-
tial intrigue with paper
as a button material was
to create buttons with
multiple layers of paper,
and buttons so light-
weight that they could
be used with the sheerest
fabrics and papers.

To make the but-
tons, handmade cotton
paper was soaked in paraf-
fin and beeswax and then
cut into button shapes. At
this point, Heather was
disappointed that the layering effect had not
worked and that the but-
tons had raw edges.
Heather held the buttons
under a bunsen burner
flame to melt the wax and
smooth out the edges,
and was pleased to discov-
er that interesting pat-
terns could be added to
the buttons with pliers.

Button designer Kimberly Shuck learned this braiding technique from a master basketmaker. "Native peoples from the North Coast of California fashion this braid from bear grass and often use it to trim dance dresses. The ribbon adds a very western feel to the braid, and I frequently use braided ribbon buttons on my children's clothes because they are so easy to make and replace and also because they are fun to look at."

To make a braided ribbon button, make a length of braid about 1/2" longer than the distance across the button, referring to the illustrations as you work. Tuck the end all the way through the loop on the last pass with the ribbon and pull the previous loop snug. Assemble the button with a fabric button covering kit, noting the braid's wrong side (the flatter side) as you work. Kimberly recommends using wired ribbon for the background fabric because it easily bends around the button mold. Dampen the fabric to make it more cooperative, and pull it tight against the button mold to prevent bunching. Tack the braid into position if you prefer it not to move around on the button. Kimberly leaves her braids untacked, and finds the buttons more interesting when the braids are positioned slightly off center.

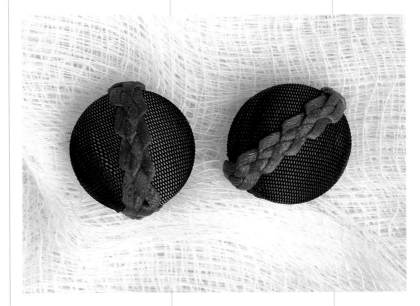

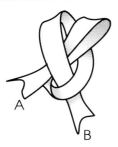

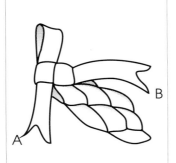

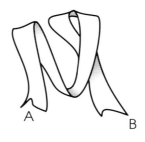

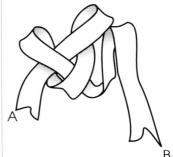

KNIT DESIGNER KATHLEEN POWER JOHNSON TAUGHT HERSELF TO MAKE TRADITIONAL DORSET BUTTONS SEVERAL YEARS AGO, BUT IT WASN'T LONG BEFORE SHE BEGAN EXPERIMENTING WITH NEW MATERIALS AND TECHNIQUES. "NEEDLEWEAVING HAS SO MANY CREATIVE POSSIBILITIES FOR BUTTONMAKING. YOU CAN MIX ELEMENTS FROM WEAVING, MACRAME, BASKETRY, TATTING, CROCHET, EMBROIDERY, AND EVEN SOME SKILLS YOU LEARNED IN KINDERGARTEN! THE *BANDOLIER BUTTON* (THE YELLOW, GREEN, AND RED BUTTON) WAS THE RESULT OF 'DOODLING' TO SEE WHAT WOULD HAPPEN IF I USED A PLAIN WEAVE ON A MINUSCULE SCALE."

NEEDLEWEAVING INVOLVES SETTING UP A WARP OF THREADS ON A FRAMEWORK AND THEN WEAVING IN A WEFT OF THREADS IN A MATCHING OR CONTRASTING COLOR. THE

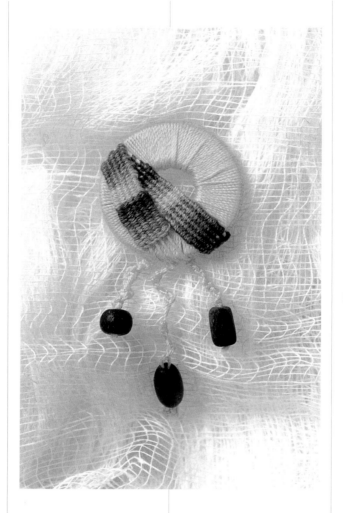

WARP IS A NETWORK OF THREADS (AS FEW AS TWO OR MORE THAN 36) WHICH ACTS AS A MATRIX FOR WEAVING. WHEN WEAVING IN THE ROUND, THE WARP THREADS LOOK LIKE THE SPOKES OF A WHEEL. IN FIBER ART BUTTONS, THE WARP MAY BE FORMED FROM A CONTINUATION OF THE WRAPPING THREAD OR BY INTRODUCING A DIFFERENT THREAD. SINGLE ROWS OF KNOTS IN THE WARP MAY BE TURNED TO THE INSIDE.

THE WEFT THREADS ARE WOVEN IN A FULL OR PARTIAL CIRCLE, DEPENDING ON THE DESIGN. THEY MAY BE INTERLACED, WRAPPED, LOOPED, KNOTTED, OR CHAINED. THE WEFT CAN BE ANY COMBINATION OF THREAD COLORS AND TEXTURES, AND IT CAN BE WOVEN AS LOOSE OR TIGHT AS DESIRED.

TO START A NEEDLEWOVEN BUTTON YOU FIRST NEED TO COVER THE BUTTON'S FRAME (A PLASTIC RING OR NYLON WASHER) WITH A LAYER OF WRAPPING THREADS. THE WRAPPING THREADS ARE USUALLY WORKED IN A SERIES OF BUTTONHOLE STITCHES (ALSO KNOWN AS HALF HITCH STITCHES) TIGHTLY AROUND THE RING. TO WORK THE STITCH, HOLD THE RING AND THE END OF THE WRAPPING THREAD IN YOUR LEFT HAND WITH THE THREAD NEXT TO THE RING. WITH THE OTHER END OF THE

THREAD IN A TAPESTRY NEE-
DLE, INSERT DOWN INTO
THE RING FROM ABOVE,
KEEPING A LOOP TO THE
RIGHT, AND THEN UNDER
THE RING AND UP INTO THE
LOOP. PULL TIGHT. TO JOIN
A NEW STRAND, PULL A NEW
THREAD THROUGH THE LAST
KNOT FORMED SO THAT IT
EMERGES FROM THE SAME
PLACE AS THE END. LEAVE A
TAIL OF 1 OR 2", THEN CON-
TINUE TO WORK THE ROW
OF KNOTS WHILE HOLDING
THE OLD END AGAINST THE
RING SO THE NEW STITCHES
ARE WORKED OVER THIS
END. ONCE THE RING IS
TIGHTLY COVERED, DOU-
BLECHECK THAT THE WRAP-
PING HAS NOT TWISTED AND
INSERT THE THREAD
THROUGH THE FIRST KNOT
IN THE RING. USE A FINE
NEEDLE TO RUN ALL THE
ENDS UNDER THE WRAPPING
THREADS. THE WARP
THREADS ARE NOW WOUND
AROUND THE ENTIRE RING.

To make *The*
Wave (THE BEIGE AND RED
BUTTON) YOU WILL NEED A
7/8" OR 1" PLASTIC RING, A
TAPESTRY NEEDLE, CROCHET
COTTON, AND SPACE-DYED
COTTON THREAD. WORK THE
BUTTONHOLE STITCH WRAP-
PING AROUND THE RING,
WITH CROCHET COTTON,
THEN CROLL THE KNOTS
BENEATH THE BUTTON. WIND
EQUALLY SPACED, PARALLEL
WARP THREADS AROUND THE
CENTER RING 7 TIMES,
ANCHORING THE KNOTTING
UNDERNEATH. ANCHOR THE
WEFT THREAD (A CONTINUA-
TION OF THE WARP THREAD)
IN THE KNOTS ON EVERY CIR-
CUIT. BEGINNING AT THE
EDGE OF THE BUTTON OPEN-
ING, WEAVE OVER AND UNDER
THE WARP THREADS FOR 5
PASSES, INCREASING THE TEN-
SION ON THE WEFT OF THE
LAST 4 PASSES TO CREATE A
GENTLE DISTORTION.

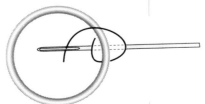

Buttonhole Stitch

**"THE BANDOLIER BUTTON…WAS THE RESULT
OF 'DOODLING' TO SEE WHAT WOULD
HAPPEN IF I USED A PLAIN WEAVING ON
A MINUSCULE SCALE."**

GEOMETRIC CLAY BUTTONS

WHEN JEWELRY DESIGN-ER TAMELA WELLS LAITY MAKES BUTTONS, SHE APPROACHES THEM WITH THE IDEA THAT THEY ARE, IN FACT, JEWELRY. TAMELA DRAWS INSPIRATION FOR HER GEOMETRIC PATTERNS FROM KALEIDOSCOPES AND PATCHWORK QUILTS, AND HER BUTTONS OFTEN TAKE ON VERY INNOVATIVE, NON-TRADITIONAL SHAPES. "I'M VERY CONSCIOUS OF THE BUTTON'S SHAPE AS I WORK. EACH CLAY PATTERN HAS A LIFE OF ITS OWN AND I JUST FOLLOW ALONG WITH IT WHEN DETERMINING THE FINISHED SHAPE."

TAMELA'S WORK-ING CYCLE BEGINS WITH SEVERAL DAYS OF MIXING CLAY COLORS, THEN TWO WEEKS OF PUTTING LOAVES TOGETHER AND MAKING PATTERNS, FOLLOWED BY A LENGTHY TIME PERIOD OF ASSEMBLING THE BAKED PIECES INTO JEWELRY. TO MAKE THE BUTTONS, TAMELA CREATES SEWING HOLES IN THE CLAY WITH A NEEDLE BEFORE BAKING, OR GLUES A PLASTIC SHANK FINDING TO THE BACK OF A BAKED BUT-TON. FOR BUTTON COVERS, YAMELA LAYS A CLAY SLICE OVER THE TOP OF A BUTTON COVER AND FORMS IT OVER THE LID. SHE THEN BAKES THE CLAY AND BUTTON COVER TOGETHER TO ENSURE A PERFECT FIT. AFTER THE CLAY COOLS, TAMELA SECURES THE TWO PIECES TOGETHER WITH GLUE.

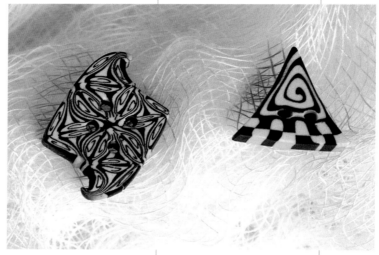

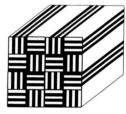

"I KEPT COMING ACROSS THESE OLD BUTTON PIECES WHILE TRAVELING," REMEMBERS JEWELRY DESIGNER MELANIE ALTER OF THE MELANIE COLLECTION, "AND WHEN I'D GET HOME EVERYONE WANTED TO BUY THEM. SOME OF THE BUTTONS ARE SEVERAL HUNDRED YEARS OLD AND OVER THE YEARS THEY HAVE BECOME HARDER AND HARDER TO COME BY, SO I DECIDED TO REPRODUCE THEM."

THE DESIGNS IN THESE PIECES ORIGINATED IN TIBET, AFGHANISTAN, SYRIA, AND NORTH INDIA (CLOCKWISE FROM THE CENTER TOP). TO MAKE THE BUTTONS, MELANIE FIRST MAKES A RUBBER MOLD FROM THE ORIGINAL PIECE. THE MOLDS ARE THEN REWORKED AND REFINED TO CORRECT ANY FLAWS OR BLEMISHES IN THE ORIGINAL BUTTON. AFTER THE BUTTONS HAVE BEEN CAST, THEY ARE TUMBLED AND THEN HAND-FINISHED.

THE DESIGNS IN THESE PIECES ORIGINATED IN TIBET, AFGHANISTAN, SYRIA, AND NORTH INDIA

WEARABLES

Technically, buttons have been "wearables" for many centuries, but not until recently have they been so creatively arranged into such an intriguing variety of wearable art works. Virtually any garment can be embellished with treasures from your button jars — hats, vests, belts, jackets, and even ties — as long as you keep a few simple guidelines in mind. If you choose to use a lot of buttons, space them with care to prevent their weight from pulling awkwardly on the garment, then tie off the threads between buttons or carry them carefully enough to prevent unsightly puckers. For button jewelry, search out your favorite buttons and then browse through this chapter for a project that will do your buttons justice.

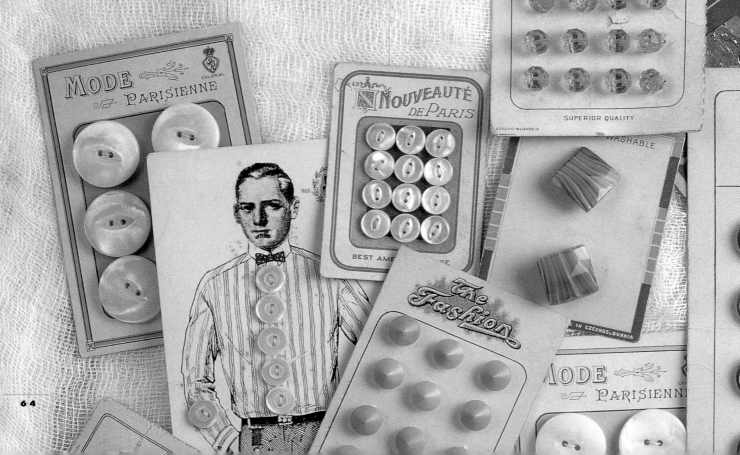

BUTTON BERET

"THIS HAT IS A COLLECTION OF BUTTON MEMORIES," EXPLAINS DESIGNER NIKI RUXTON. "I HAVE BEEN COLLECTING BUTTONS FROM OLD GARMENTS — STORING THEM IN ANTIQUE TINS FOR YEARS — WAITING FOR A QUIET MOMENT OF INSPIRATION." AS SHE SEWED THE BUTTONS ON, NIKI VIEWED THE BERET AS A WEARABLE CANVAS. "THE BERET IS POWERFUL TO WEAR; IT MAKES A STATEMENT OF MY PERSONALITY AND CAPTURES THE ATTENTION OF OTHERWISE-CASUAL OBSERVERS."

H E A R T   P I N   A N D   P U R S E

THIS CHARMING PURSE STARTED OUT AS A VEST, BUT SOMETHING WENT WRONG IN THE ASSEMBLY PROCESS SO WEARABLE ART DESIGNER CHRISTEN BROWN WHITTLED IT DOWN TO A PURSE. THE PIN WAS FORMED OVER A CARDBOARD CUTOUT BASE WITH A LEATHER PIECE AND PIN BACKING GLUED TO THE BACK SIDE. "IT TOOK EVERY LAST SCRAP OF FABRIC I HAD FOR THE PIN," LAUGHS CHRISTEN, "DOWN TO THE LAST HALF INCH." TO ATTACH THE FABRIC SCRAPS, CHRISTEN USED A WATER-SOLUBLE STABLEIZER. THE BUTTONS WERE ADDED LAST.

"MAMA'S BUTTON JAR"

"I'M NOT FOND OF WORKING WITH CHIFFON," SAYS CLOTHING DESIGNER MARTHA RICHARD, "BUT NOTHING ELSE GAVE ME THE EFFECT I WANTED FOR THE JARS." TO MAKE THE JACKET, MARTHA FIRST CREATED JAR PATTERNS ON TISSUE PAPER, TRYING TO REPLICATE THE SHAPES AND SIZES OF HER GRANDMOTHER'S BUTTON JARS. AFTER MARKING THE JAR POSITIONS ON THE UNLINED JACKET, MARTHA BEGAN SEWING ON THE BUTTONS. TO DUPLICATE THE WAY BUTTONS SETTLE IN JARS, MARTHA PLACED THE LARGER, HEAVIER BUTTONS IN THE BOTTOM AREAS AND

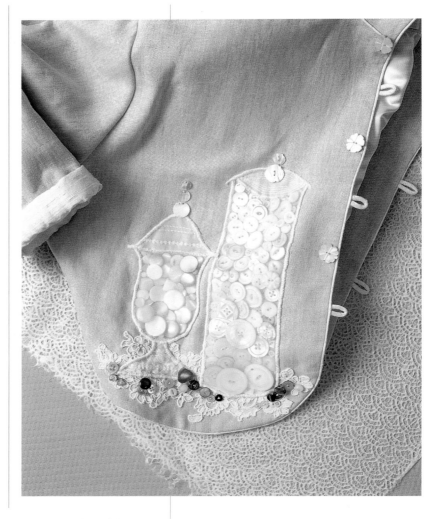

"MANY OF THE BUTTONS ARE ACTUALLY FROM MY GRANDMOTHER'S BUTTON JARS, AND I DELIBERATELY DID NOT CLEAN THEM BECAUSE I LIKED THEIR TIME-WEATHERED LOOK."

THE SMALLER, LIGHTER BUTTONS ON TOP. "MANY OF THE BUTTONS ARE ACTUALLY FROM MY GRANDMOTHER'S BUTTON JARS, AND I DELIBERATELY DID NOT CLEAN THEM BECAUSE I LIKED THEIR TIME-WEATHERED LOOK." AFTER ALL THE BUTTONS WERE SEWN ON, MARTHA HAND-STITCHED THE CHIFFON JAR SHAPES OVER THE BUTTONS, AND THEN FINISHED BY LINING THE JACKET.

B U T T O N   J A C K E T

SEAMSTRESS MARTHA RICHARD HAS BEEN ACQUIRING BUTTONS FROM FRIENDS, RELATIVES, AND TRAVELS FOR A LONG TIME. A FEW YEARS AGO, ABOUT THE TIME SHE DECIDED TO ORGANIZE THE BUTTONS, MARTHA CAME ACROSS A LENGTH OF 1960'S WINDOWPANE DENIM AND DECIDED TO MAKE SOMETHING FROM IT. THE TWO IDEAS CAME TOGETHER, AND SEW THE BUTTONS, BUT IT WAS ALL WORTH IT BECAUSE I LOVE THE COMMENTS PEOPLE MAKE WHEN I WEAR THE JACKET."

THE JACKET CONTAINS MORE THAN 500 BUTTONS, WITH MANY OF THEM REMINISCENT OF SPECIAL TIMES AND PLACES.

AND THE BUTTON JACKET SOON BECAME A WEARABLE ART PIECE ENTITLED *BUTTON, BUTTON, WHO'S GOT THE BUTTON? I DO!*

THE JACKET CONTAINS MORE THAN 500 BUTTONS, WITH MANY OF THEM REMINISCENT OF SPECIAL TIMES AND PLACES. MARTHA ADMITS THAT SEWING ON THE BUTTONS WAS THE LEAST ENJOYABLE ASPECT OF THE PROJECT. "IT TOOK THREE TEN-HOUR DAYS TO ARRANGE

EMBELLISHED SHIRT

WHEN MULTIMEDIA ARTIST GARY LEIDNER FIRST SAT DOWN WITH NEEDLE, THREAD, AND A FEW WHITE BUTTONS, HIS ONLY INTENTION WAS TO ADD LIFE TO A FADING DENIM SHIRT. ONCE HE STARTED, THOUGH, HE JUST COULDN'T STOP. GARY SEWED THE SMALLER BUTTONS IN PLACE FIRST AND THEN FILLED IN THE GAPS WITH THE LARGER BUTTONS, ALLOWING THEM TO OVERLAP. THE ASYMMETRICAL ACCENTS ON THE COLLAR, POCKETS, AND CUFFS JUST SORT OF EVOLVED. "THAT'S THE NICE PART ABOUT WORKING WITH BUTTONS," GARY SAYS. "YOU DON'T HAVE TO FOLLOW A SPECIFIC DESIGN — JUST KEEP ADDING BUTTONS UNTIL YOU'RE HAPPY WITH THE LOOK." FOR ADDED STYLE, GARY THREADED SEVERAL 4" LENGTHS OF FINE WIRE WITH AN ASSORTMENT OF BEADS IN COMPATIBLE COLORS AND ATTACHED THEM TO THE SHIRT BY INSERTING ONE END OF THE WIRE THROUGH A BUTTON'S

"YOU DON'T HAVE TO FOLLOW A SPECIFIC DESIGN — JUST KEEP ADDING BUTTONS UNTIL YOU'RE HAPPY WITH THE LOOK."

SEWING HOLES AND THEN LOOPING IT BACK THROUGH AND TWISTING TO SECURE.

EMBELLISHED CLOTHING

"FOR AS LONG AS I CAN REMEMBER," LAMENTS BUTTON LOVER MARY SAVAGE, "EVERYONE HAS GIVEN ME SUCH A HARD TIME ABOUT MY BUTTONS. AT LEAST MY

"AT LEAST MY HUSBAND HAS FINALLY LEARNED TO LIVE WITH JARS OF BUTTONS ALL OVER THE HOUSE."

HUSBAND HAS FINALLY LEARNED TO LIVE WITH JARS OF BUTTONS ALL OVER THE HOUSE."

MARY USES MANY OF HER BUTTONS TO EMBELLISH CLOTHING, WHICH SHE SELLS AT CRAFT FAIRS. SHE USES PRIMARILY OLDER BUTTONS, PREFERRING THEIR IMPERFECTIONS AND INTRIGUING DETAILS. "PEOPLE MUST THINK OF SEWING ON BUTTONS AS VERY TIME-CONSUMING WORK, BECAUSE THEY FREQUENTLY ASK IF I TIE OFF THE THREAD BETWEEN EACH BUTTON." (ACTUALLY, MARY CARRIES THE THREADS BEHIND THE BUTTONS.)

BUTTON VESTS

Wearable artist Christen Brown credits her early playtime in the family button box as the origin of her interest in color and design. "I would spend hours

"I ENJOY USING BUTTONS AS EMBELLISHMENT INSTEAD OF FOR THEIR PRACTICAL FUNCTION."

arranging different colors of buttons together, and I started seeing color in a totally new way." Christen's vests feature buttons of all types. "I enjoy using them as embellishment instead of for their practical function." Some of Christen's buttons are sewn on with decorative beads, while others are wired in clusters onto small pieces of fine chicken wire and then sewn on as a single piece.

When she lectures to quilt and embroidery guilds, Christen likes to share the story of how she acquired some of her buttons. "One day, when I was working in a co-op gallery, a woman noticed my vests and said, 'Now I know who to give my button collection to.' I didn't pay much attention to her comment at the time, but when I worked my next shift there were eight boxes of buttons waiting for me. The buttons are true treasures, and I would love to thank the giver but she didn't leave her name and never returned to the gallery."

B U T T O N   T I E

"To be honest," confesses clothing designer Mary Savage, "ties were initially just something else to put buttons on." For this piece, Mary embellished one of a friend's hand-painted ties. "It is slightly more

"YOU HAVE TO FIND BUTTONS THAT ECHO THE FABRIC'S DESIGN — INSTEAD OF COMPETING WITH IT…"

complicated than just sewing on buttons, though. You have to find buttons that echo the fabric's design — instead of competing with it — and you have to be careful to distribute the buttons so their weight doesn't affect the way the tie hangs."

BUTTON EARRINGS

Jewelry designer Kimberley Adams uses a variety of jewelry findings (the hardware used to make jewelry) and inexpensive, coordinating buttons and beads to make button earrings. "Don't be disappointed if it takes some playing around to get a design you like," advises Kimberley. "Sometimes, the buttons sitting next to each other in the button box are the perfect combination for a pair of earrings, while other times I have to thread and unthread lots of buttons to achieve the right look."

Kimberley recommends T-pins, French ear wire, and clip earring bases as the findings of choice. Insert one end of a 6" length of wire (brass or stainless steel) through one of a button's sewing holes.

Thread the wire through about 1/2" and twist tightly to secure. Drop a large bead onto the wire and press it down to cover the twisted wire, then add smaller beads as desired. Make a loop just above the last bead and cut off any excess wire. Gently open the small Frendh ear wire loop and drop your strand of beads and buttons onto the wire. Kimberley notes that it takes practice to get the wire twisted right and that a good pair of small pliers can make your work easier. For earrings with multiple drops, look for French ear wires specially designed to accommodate a drop.

To use a shank button, thread a T-pin through the shank and then glue it in place. When the glue has completely dried, form a loop

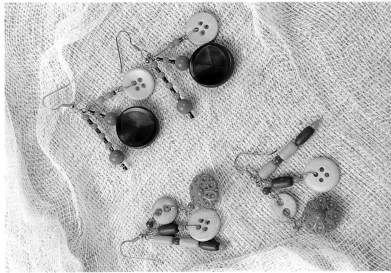

in the top of the T-pin and hang it on a French ear wire loop. For clip-on earrings, simply snip the shank off the back of a button and glue its back to the flat surface of a clip-on finding.

CROCHETED
BUTTON NECKLACE

AILEEN GUGENHEIM'S CROCHETED BUTTON NECKLACES NEVER TIRE AS CONVERSATION PIECES. TO THE FREQUENTLY ASKED QUESTION OF WHERE SHE GETS ALL THE BUTTONS, AILEEN CONFESSES TO HAVING A SON-IN-LAW IN THE INDUSTRIAL RAG BUSINESS WHO GENEROUSLY SHARES BUTTONS THAT HAVE BEEN REMOVED FROM SHREDDED CLOTHING. FOR THE ANTIQUE BUTTONS INTERMINGLED IN HER WORK, AILEEN RELIES ON A FRIEND WHO PICKS THEM UP FOR HER AS SHE'S TRAVELING AROUND THE COUNTRY DOING ANTIQUE SHOWS. ANOTHER FREQUENT QUESTION — "HOW DO YOU FASTEN IT?" — ELICITS GREAT CHUCKLES FROM AILEEN. "WITH A BUTTON, OF COURSE!"

AILEEN BEGAN MAKING THE NECKLACES SEVERAL YEARS AGO WHEN AN OLDER FRIEND GAVE HER

ONE AS A GIFT. AS AILEEN SAYS, "I COULDN'T KEEP MY HANDS OFF IT, AND IT FELT SO GOOD AGAINST MY SKIN." SOON SHE WAS MAKING THEM HERSELF, USING HER GRANDMOTHER'S STEEL CROCHET HOOKS AND EXPERIMENTING WITH STITCHES AND PLACEMENT UNTIL SHE FOUND A LOOK SHE LIKED.

EACH NECKLACE BEGINS WITH A LENGTH OF CROCHETED CHAIN AND SINGLE CROCHET STITCHES. SMALLER BUTTONS ARE ADDED WITH LOOPS (SEE PHOTO) ON THE ENDS, WITH PROGRESSIVELY LARGER AND MORE BUTTONS WORKING UP TO THE CENTER, FOR A TOTAL OF 250 TO 350 BUTTONS PER NECKLACE. AILEEN HAS GIVEN SEVERAL WORKSHOPS TO TEACH THE TECHNIQUE. "THE CROCHET PORTION IS EXTREMELY SIMPLE, BUT MANY PEOPLE GIVE UP LONG BEFORE THEY HAVE ENOUGH BUTTONS ON FOR A NECKLACE. I GUESS I'LL TEACH BRACELETS INSTEAD FOR THE NEXT SEMINAR."

THE JINGLE FACTOR

BUTTON DESIGNER CHRISTEN BROWN HAS MANY CHILDHOOD BUTTON MEMORIES, BUT BY FAR THE MOST VIVID ARE THE DAYS WHEN SHE WAS HOME SICK IN BED, HER BODY HOT WITH FEVER, AND HER MOM WOULD BRING HER A BOX OF BUTTONS. "THE BUTTONS FELT SO COOL AGAINST MY HOT FINGERS, AND I JUST LOVED THE SOUNDS THEY MADE AS I RAN MY FINGERS THROUGH THE BOX."

CHRISTEN STILL LOVES BUTTON SOUNDS AND ENJOYS CREATING BUTTON JEWELRY THAT EMPLOYS "THE JINGLE FACTOR." REMINISCENT OF THE BUTTON BRACELETS YOUNG GIRLS WOULD MAKE IN THE 18TH CENTURY, CHRISTEN CREATED THIS NECKLACE BY WIRING CLUSTERS OF BUTTONS ONTO SMALL SCRAPS OF FINE CHICKEN WIRE AND THEN WIRING THE CLUSTERS ONTO A CHAIN NECKLACE.

"THE BUTTONS FELT SO COOL AGAINST MY HOT FINGERS, AND I JUST LOVED THE SOUNDS THEY MADE AS I RAN MY FINGERS THROUGH THE BOX."

BUTTON BROOCHES

Kathy Gillespie recommends these buckle brooches as good projects for beginning button jewelry makers. Kathy's brooches tend to be a long time in the making, since she likes to use buttons that are connected by a specific theme, such as women's faces, gargoyles, or natural motifs. Button collectors, who often scorn button crafts, appreciate her work because the glue can be soaked off without damaging the buttons.

 Kathy uses antique shoe buckles (usually sold in pairs in antique shops) as bases, and she simply arranges and glues the buttons to the surface. To create the backing, Kathy covers the buckle's back side with a layer of low temperature hot glue thick enough to fill in all the surface spaces. Next, she cuts out a piece of felt to fit the buckle back. She then inserts a pin backing through the center of the felt and marks the entrance and exit areas with an ink pen. She then removes the pin backing, hole punches the spots marked in ink, and reinserts the pin backing. To finish, Kathy covers the back side of the felt with a layer of glue and presses it against the back side of the buckle.

BUTTON JEWELRY

DESIGNER KATHLEEN HONAN, WHO HAS ALWAYS BEEN A PASSIONATE COLLECTOR OF BUTTONS AND FABRIC SCRAPS — MUCH TO THE ANNOYANCE OF FAMILY MEMBERS — IS THRILLED TO HAVE FINALLY FOUND A USE FOR ALL HER PARAPHERNALIA. "MAKING BUTTON JEWELRY GIVES ME A JUSTIFICATION TO INDULGE MY COMPULSIVE NEED TO BUY MORE DOODADS." FOR BASES, KATHLEEN USES THE BACKS OF OLD WATCH FACES (QUARTZES REMOVED), ANTIQUE COMPACT MIRRORS, AND STAINED GLASS PIECES, AS WELL AS SIMPLE MIRROR SHAPES FOUND IN CRAFT STORES. KATHLEEN ISN'T PARTICULAR ABOUT WHICH TYPES OF BUTTONS SHE USES. "I'M JUST INTRIGUED WITH INTERESTING COMBINATIONS OF COLORS AND MATERIALS." KATHLEEN SECURES THE BUTTONS AND PIN BACKINGS WITH AN EPOXY ADHESIVE.

"MAKING BUTTON JEWELRY GIVES ME A JUSTIFICATION TO INDULGE MY COMPULSIVE NEED TO BUY MORE DOODADS."

BRACELETS
AND WATCH BANDS

Just running her fingers through her collection of antique and collectible buttons provides designer Margaret W. Reed with inspiration. Like many artists, Margaret laments that

...SHE FINALLY AGREED TO SELL A CUSTOMER ONE OF HER PERSONAL BRACELETS WITH THE CONDITION THAT SHE COULD FIRST REMOVE FOUR OF HER FAVORITE BUTTONS.

customers often fall in love with her personal pieces. One such customer hounded her so frequently — "everything has a price," he kept insisting — that she finally agreed to sell him one of her personal bracelets with the condition that she could first remove four of her favorite buttons.

To make a bracelet, Margaret stitches a 7 or 8" length of sewing elastic together and then sews on a base coat of shankless buttons. Margaret uses carpet and upholstery threads for their durability. After the base coat, Margaret adds more and more layers of interesting buttons, "junking them up," as she calls this stage.

Although Margaret prefers the whimsical effect of bracelets large enough to slide up and down the wearer's arm, a more fitted bracelet can be custom made by adding 1/2" to the intended wearer's wrist measurement for a seam allowance and another 1/2 to 3/4" to compensate for the tightening that occurs when the buttons are sewn on.

For a watch band, Margaret first adds 1/2 to 3/4" to the wrist measurement for ease, and then another 2" for foldover allowance. She takes the watch face with her when she shops for elastic and purchases one that fits easily through the band loops. She then inserts the elastic ends through the band loops, folds the elastic over 1" with the fold on the outside edge, and topstitches to secure. (The fold will be covered with buttons and won't show in the finished project.) Last, Margaret covers the elastic as she would for a bracelet.

COLOR DISPLAYS

"I like a lot of color," admits button jewelry designer Mary McClaren. "Working as an architect, I have to wear primarily black clothing so on my off time I'm like a kid with color." Mary's attraction to color may also be attributed partly to the time she spent living in the tropics, where "color is so intense and such a delight to the eye." Mary found the large orange button in a bin full of '40's buttons in a shop in Haiti and was immediately attracted to its bright color. Mary forms her jewelry over ready-to-decorate metal pin bases (found in jewelry making supply shops). She adds the buttons in layers, securing them with glue or prismatic color wires that show in the finished pieces.

"WORKING AS AN ARCHITECT, I HAVE TO WEAR PRIMARILY BLACK CLOTHING SO ON MY OFF TIME I'M LIKE A KID WITH COLOR."

BUTTON NECKLACE

Necklace designer Bee Hill made this necklace to wear to an international bead conference. "I knew that everyone there would be wearing beads, and I wanted something different." Bee strung shank buttons on tiger tail wire and pulled the buttons up tightly for a clustered effect. She then threaded crimp beads and closing hooks onto the wire ends, trimmed the wire ends to 3/4", threaded the wire back through the crimp bead, and crimped it securely in place. In choosing buttons for the necklace, Bee took the advice of an old friend. "Watch the Chinese," she often said, "They always use a little sparkle."

CLASSIC LAYERS

"THERE TEND TO BE ONLY TWO DESIGN SCHOOLS WITH BUTTON JEWELRY," EXPLAINS MULTIMEDIA ARTIST VICKI FOX. "EITHER YOU CLUSTER THE BUTTONS OR YOU STACK THEM. I BELIEVE EACH BUTTON SHOULD BE SEEN, SO I'M DEFINITELY FROM THE STACKING SCHOOL." VICKI'S FASCINATION WITH BUTTONS BEGAN AT AN EARLY AGE. HER MOTHER'S UNCLE OWNED A BUTTON FACTORY, AND WHEN THE FACTORY CLOSED, MANY OF THE BUTTONS WENT TO VICKI'S MOTHER. "ON RAINY DAYS," VICKI REMEMBERS, "MY SISTER AND I WOULD SPEND HOURS STRINGING MATCHING BUTTONS TOGETHER."

EVEN WITH HER LARGE BUTTON COLLECTION, IT'S STILL DIFFICULT TO FIND SHAPES THAT WILL "SIT WELL TOGETHER," AND THEN THERE ARE THE ADDED COMPLICATIONS OF COLOR AND STYLE. VICKI USES A SILICONE INDUS-TRIAL-GRADE GLUE TO JOIN THE BUTTON LAYERS AND THE PIN BACKINGS. "BECAUSE THE INDIVIDUAL BUTTONS THAT MAKE UP THE PIECES ARE SUCH DISPARATE MATERIALS, THEY EXPAND AND CONTRACT AT DIFFERENT RATES, AND THE SILICONE IS THE ONLY ADHE-SIVE I'VE FOUND THAT IS FLEXIBLE ENOUGH TO ACCOM-MODATE THE CHANGES."

VICKI SELLS HER PIECES AT CRAFT SHOWS AND BOU-TIQUES, AND HER WORK ATTRACTS WOMEN, MEN, AND CHILDREN ALIKE, AND VIRTU-ALLY EVERYONE HAS A STORY ABOUT PLAYING IN THEIR GRANDMOTHER'S BUTTON BOX. "WHEN THE CHILDREN ARE TEMPTED BY THE JEWELRY AND START TOUCHING IT, I DIRECT THEM TO A CIGAR BOX OF ASSORTED BUTTONS AND CHALLENGE THEM TO FIND FIVE BUTTONS THAT MATCH.

"ON RAINY DAYS," VICKI REMEMBERS, "MY SISTER AND I WOULD SPEND HOURS STRINGING MATCHING BUTTONS TOGETHER."

BY THE TIME THEY FIND FIVE MATCHING BUTTONS," VICKI LAUGHS, "MOM HAS USUALLY HAD ENOUGH TIME TO DECIDE ON A PIECE."

ALTHOUGH DESIGNER DIANE GRINNELL ADMITS TO BEING TEMPTED BY THE GLUE GUN FOR THESE PROJECTS, SHE RESISTED. "I GUESS I'M JUST A PURIST," SHE SAYS. "AND BESIDES, SEWING THEM WITH A SPECIAL THREAD ADDS ONE MORE LAYER OF INTEREST."

TO MAKE THE SCARF CLIP, DIANE THREADED SATIN CORDING THROUGH THE SEWING HOLES OF AN OVERSIZED BUTTON AND THEN TIED THE CORDING TO THE CLIP WITH SEVERAL SQUARE KNOTS. (LOOK FOR SCARF CLIP HARDWARE IN THE CRAFT SECTION OF LARGER FABRIC STORES.) TO AVOID FRAYING ENDS, DIANE THREADED THE CORDING THROUGH AN EMBROIDERY NEEDLE AND WORKED THE ENDS INTO THE KNOTS.

TO MAKE EACH HAT PIN, DIANE INSERTED A LONG HAT PIN THROUGH THE CENTER OF A 3/4"

SQUARE OF SATIN FABRIC. WHEN THE FABRIC REACHED THE PEARL-TIPPED END, DIANE FOLDED THE EDGES UP AND OVER THE PEARL. SHE STITCHED THE FABRIC TOGETHER AND THEN FOLDED THE RAW EDGES INSIDE AND TACKED THEM DOWN TO CREATE A PADDED SURFACE. TO FINISH, DIANE EXPERIMENTED WITH PLACEMENT ANGLES AND THEN STITCHED AN ANTIQUE LEAF BUTTON TO THE FABRIC, USING A GREEN SILK BUTTONHOLE TWIST TO ACCENTUATE THE LEAF SHAPE.

EASY GLAMOUR

DESIGNER DIANE GRINNELL HAS ALWAYS BEEN INTERESTED IN BUTTONS. "AS A SEWER, I WAS ALWAYS MORE INTRIGUED WITH FINDING EXCITING CLOSURES THAN IN DESIGNING COMPLICATED GARMENT CONSTRUCTIONS." TO MAKE THE SHOE CLIPS AND CUFF LINKS, DIANE COVERED METAL FINDINGS WITH SQUARES OF SATIN FABRIC, FOLDED THE EDGES IN TOWARD THE CENTER, AND BLINDSTITCHED THE RAW EDGES UNDER. TO FINISH, DIANE STITCHED THE BUTTONS TO THE PADDED FABRIC SURFACE BY THE FABRIC. NOTE: ALTHOUGH FINDINGS USUALLY COME WITH PRECUT SEWING HOLES, DIANE RECOMMENDS COVERING THEM WITH FABRIC TO PREVENT THE RAW METAL EDGES FROM DAMAGING SHOES OR CLOTHING.

EMBELLISHMENTS

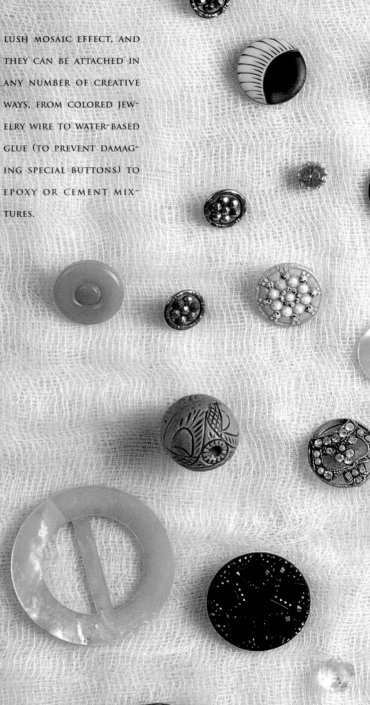

After thousands of years of dutiful service as practical clothing closures, buttons are finally getting some respect. From handmade paper makers to sculptors, from bookbinders to doll makers, artists from a wide range of disciplines are discovering the versatility of buttons. A quick browse through this chapter will reveal some of the more interesting possibilities, and who knows what seeds of inspiration their work may plant in your subconscious. (One designer professes a strong desire to cover her time-weathered refrigerator with buttons.) Buttons can be showcased as cherished individuals or clustered together to create a lush mosaic effect, and they can be attached in any number of creative ways, from colored jewelry wire to water-based glue (to prevent damaging special buttons) to epoxy or cement mixtures.

PULLMAN

THE BUTTON KING

THE QUESTION OF "WHY?" FREQUENTLY PASSES THE LIPS OF PEOPLE WHO SEE DALTON STEVEN'S WORK. "IT DID SEEM KIND OF WEIRD AT FIRST," ADMITS DALTON, WHO STARTED ATTACHING BUTTONS TO THINGS IN 1983. "I HAVE INSOMNIA, AND I USED TO CLEAN THE HOUSE AT NIGHT WHILE EVERYONE ELSE SLEPT JUST TO HAVE SOMETHING TO DO. BUT YOU CAN ONLY CLEAN A HOUSE SO MANY TIMES. ONE NIGHT I STARTED SEWING BUTTONS ONTO A SUIT, AND I HAVEN'T STOPPED SINCE." DALTON WORKED ON THE SUIT FOR 34 MONTHS, AND PROUDLY POINTS OUT THAT IT (AND THE COORDINATING CAP) HAS 16,333 BUTTONS AND WEIGHS 16.1 POUNDS. DALTON HAS DIS-COVERED THAT BUTTON PEO-PLE ARE VERY GENEROUS. WHEN HE FIRST BEGAN WORKING WITH BUTTONS, HE WROTE TO THE ADELPHIA

"ONE NIGHT I STARTED SEWING BUTTONS ONTO
A SUIT, AND I HAVEN'T STOPPED SINCE."

BUTTON COMPANY AND
ASKED IF HE COULD PUR-
CHASE BUTTONS AT WHOLE-
SALE RATES. THE COMPANY
ASKED HIM TO SEND PHOTOS
OF HIS WORK AND LATER
SENT HIM SEVERAL DRUMS
OF FREE BUTTONS; DALTON
HAD SIMILAR LUCK WITH
THE MANUFACTURER OF THE
CONTACT CEMENT HE USES
TO ADHERE THE BUTTONS.
WHEN DALTON WENT TO
JAPAN TO ENTERTAIN THE
IRIS BUTTON COMPANY
WITH HIS MUSIC AND BUT-
TONS, THEY SENT HIM
50,000 BUTTONS. AND
AFTER DALTON GRACED THE
COVER OF A CHILDREN'S
BOOK, STUDENTS FROM ALL
OVER THE COUNTRY SENT
BUTTONS TO HIM.

DALTON'S FASCI-
NATION WITH BUTTONS HAS
GENERATED MANY INTEREST-
ING OPPORTUNITIES. HE HAS
APPEARED ON MANY TALK
SHOWS (DAVID LETTERMAN,
JOHNNY CARSON, AND THE
TODAY SHOW, TO MENTION
JUST A FEW), TRAVELED TO
FAIRS ACROSS THE UNITED

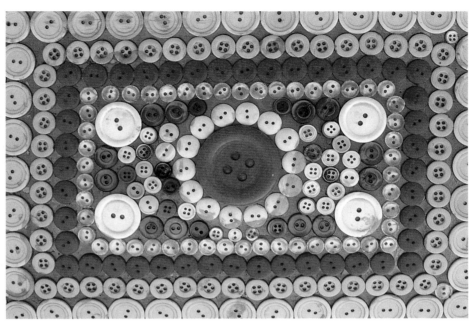

STATES AND CANADA, BEEN LISTED IN THE GUINNESS BOOK OF WORLD RECORDS, AND APPEARED IN THE MOVIE WILD WHEELS. DALTON ENJOYS VISITS FROM SIGHTSEERS FROM AS FAR AWAY AS AFRICA.

WHEN DALTON'S INSOMNIA REACHED THE POINT WHERE HE SAW DEATH AS AN IMMINENT POSSIBILITY, HE BEGAN WORKING ON THE COFFIN AND HEARSE. "THE HEARSE IS COVERED WITH MORE THAN 600,000 BUTTONS, AND IS GOING TO CARRY ME WHEN I GO," SAYS DALTON. DALTON IS NOT PICKY ABOUT THE TYPES OF BUTTONS HE USES — "AS LONG AS THEY'RE FLAT." DALTON'S WORK-IN-PROGRESS INCLUDES AN ALL-BUTTON OUTHOUSE, WHICH HE PLANS TO OUTFIT WITH A BUTTON-COVERED TOILET.

WHEN DALTON'S INSOMNIA REACHED THE POINT WHERE HE SAW DEATH AS AN IMMINENT POSSIBILITY, HE BEGAN WORKING ON THE COFFIN AND HEARSE.

Brenna Busse made her first dolls by wrapping scraps of her old clothing around sticks. She slept with the dolls at night, mimicking the fertility doll traditions of other cultures. "Those first dolls were my prayers to have a child." Within a year Brenna had given birth to a daughter.

▬▬▬ Since her daughter's birth, Brenna has made hundreds of dolls, many of them using recycled objects such as springs, zippers, and buttons. "The buttons become like shields of armor on these images. With the *Pearly Princess*, the shield of pearls is my visual response to the stories about the pearly kings and queens in England." (Pearlies were the street vendors around the turn of the century who deco-

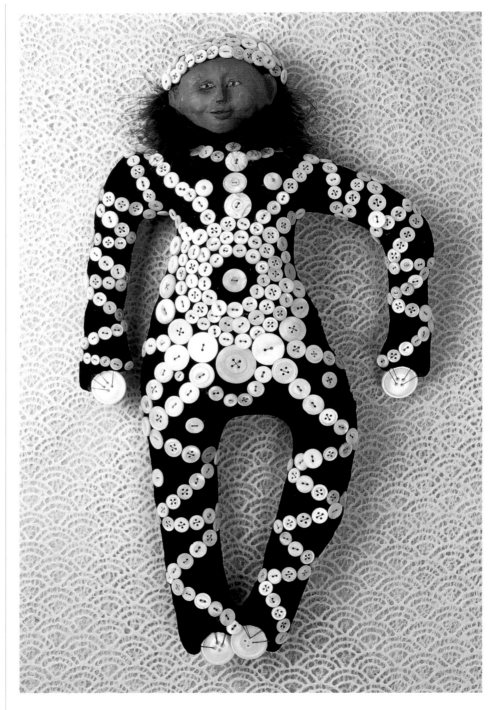

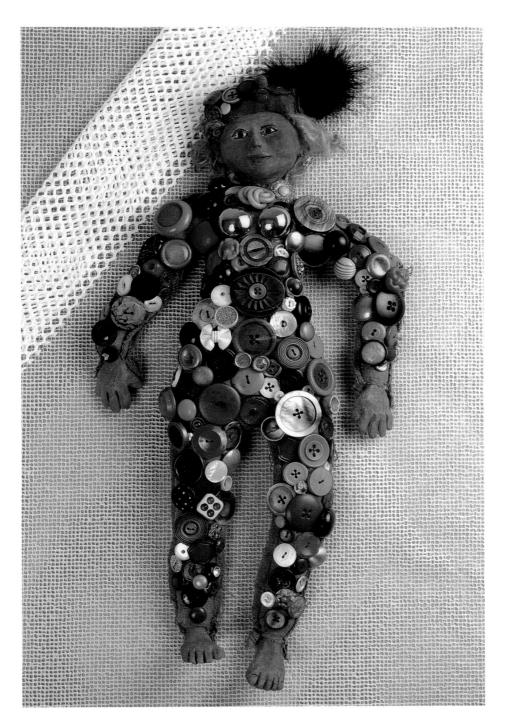

"WITH THE PEARLY PRINCESS, THE SHIELD OF PEARLS IS MY VISUAL RESPONSE TO THE STORIES ABOUT THE PEARLY KINGS AND QUEENS IN ENGLAND."

RATED THEIR BLACK SUITS AND DRESSES WITH PEARLY BUTTONS WITH VERY DRAMATIC RESULTS.) "I THINK ABOUT THE BUTTONS AS I SEW THEM ON . . . ABOUT THE UNIQUENESS OF EACH ONE AND ABOUT MY GRANDMOTHER'S BUTTON CANS."

"It took a long time to find just the right buttons for these stockings," says designer Mary Savage. "All of the buttons I tried just didn't look right." Soon after, Mary received a surprise call from a stranger who had read about her work with vintage buttons, asking if Mary would like her grandmother's button collection. (The caller had planned to give the buttons to a local charity for kids to make craft projects from.)

"I went to the caller's house and she showed me lots of pictures of her grandmother, told me stories about her, and then gave me the buttons. When she saw how excited I was, she pulled out her mother's collection of '50s buttons and gave me those also. I was really thrilled because it's gotten harder and harder to find these types of buttons, and they looked perfect on the stockings."

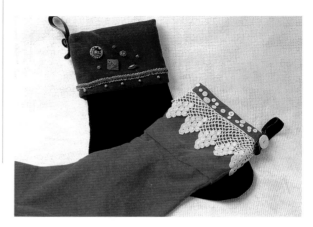

SHOOTING STARS

Textile artist and surface designer Diane Grinnell created these button napkin rings to embellish her collection of cotton damask dinner napkins. To form the rings, Diane marked off 6" lengths of gold cording and green and burgundy cording, wrapped masking tape around the marked areas, and cut the lengths apart through the middle of the masking tape. (The tape helps prevent fraying.) Next, Diane twisted the gold cording around the green and burgundy to form one, three-color length. She then brought the two taped ends together and tacked them together at four or five points with a double-stranded thread. To cover the raw edges and form a surface to sew the but-

tons onto, Diane cut out a 1-1/2- x 2" piece of coordinating fabric, pressed the edges down 1/8", and folded it around the taped areas. To finish, she positioned the overlap so it will be on the inside of the napkin ring, blindstitched the layers together, and sewed on the button.

BUTTON HAT BANDS

DESIGNER KIMBERLEY ADAMS CREATED THESE BUTTON HAT BANDS AS A VERSATILE WAY TO MIX AND MATCH BUTTON ARRANGEMENTS WITH A VARIETY OF HATS. TO BEGIN, KIMBERLEY CUT A STRIP OF STURDY FABRIC 4 INCHES WIDE X THE DISTANCE AROUND THE HAT PLUS 1/2" FOR EASE AND REINFORCED IT WITH FUSIBLE INTERFACING.

"THE NEXT STEPS GO QUICKLY," SAYS KIMBERLEY. FOLD THE FABRIC IN HALF LENGTHWISE WITH RIGHT SIDES FACING AND STITCH TO FORM A TUBE. TURN RIGHT SIDES OUT, WHIPSTITCH THE ENDS UNDER, AND PRESS WELL. TACK THE ENDS TOGETHER TO FORM A CIRCLE AND TRY IT ON THE HAT TO MAKE SURE IT FITS WELL.

SELECT THE BUTTONS YOU PLAN TO USE, MIXING AN APPEALING VARIETY OF SHAPES, COLORS, AND TEXTURES. SEW THE BUTTONS ONTO THE BAND WITH EMBROIDERY FLOSS, THREADING BEADS ONTO THE FLOSS OCCASIONALLY IF DESIRED. LAST, COVER THE TACKED ENDS WITH SEVERAL BUTTONS OR A LARGE SILK FLOWER.

BUTTON FABRIC VEST

"WHEN I BEGAN THIS PROJECT, I WAS INTRIGUED WITH THE IDEA OF WORKING WITH WIRE AND BUTTONS INSTEAD OF WITH FABRIC AND THREAD," SAYS CLOTHING DESIGNER MARY SAVAGE. "I WANTED TO CREATE A SCULPTURE INSTEAD OF A GARMENT." MARY'S INITIAL PLANS HAD TO BE ADAPTED, THOUGH, WHEN SHE WENT SHOPPING FOR MATERIALS. "THE HARDWARE STORE DOES NOT HAVE THE SAME VARIETY OF WIRE COLORS THAT FABRIC STORES HAVE IN FABRICS AND THREAD, AND THE ONLY WIRE THAT WAS PLIABLE ENOUGH TO FORM A THREE-DIMENSIONAL PIECE WAS BRIGHT GREEN!"

TO BEGIN, MARY MADE A PATTERN AND CUT OUT THE WIRE AS IF IT WERE FABRIC. THEN SHE WIRED THE PIECES INTO A VEST SHAPE WITH PLIERS. "I HAD TO LET GO OF MY INITIAL DESIGN AT THIS POINT BECAUSE I'D HOPED TO ADD FITTING DARTS IN THE BACK AND SOME OTHER DETAILING, BUT IT JUST WOULDN'T WORK." AT THE HALFWAY POINT, MARY ADMITS TO NOTHING LESS THAN HATRED FOR THE VEST, BUT SHE CONTINUED WORKING. "AS BUTTONS COVERED MORE AND MORE OF THE SURFACE, I BEGAN SEEING THE BUTTONS AS THE FABRIC, AND THE VEST BECAME MORE INTERESTING. SINCE I WAS USING BUTTONS AS THE FABRIC, IT MADE SENSE TO USE WIRE FOR THE BUTTONS AND BUTTON HOLES."

BUTTON BOXES

DESIGNER KIMBERLEY ADAMS CREATED THESE BUTTON BOXES AS DECORATIVE PLACES TO STASH BEDSIDE KNICKKNACKS. TO BEGIN, KIMBERLEY GROUPED HER BUTTONS IN AN APPEALING COLOR RANGE AND ADDED A FEW COLLECTED TRINKETS SUCH AS COORDINATING BEADS. NEXT, SHE REMOVED ANY BUTTON SHANKS WITH WIRE CUTTERS.

KIMBERLEY BEGAN BY GLUING BUTTONS TO THE TOP AND SIDE SURFACES OF THE LID, ALLOWING SOME OF THE BUTTONS TO DANGLE OVER THE EDGE. WITH THE BOX LID ON, KIMBERLEY LIGHTLY TRACED WITH A PENCIL THE AREA WHERE THE OUTER EDGE OF THE LID AND THE BUTTONS MET THE BOX. SHE REMOVED THE LID, SET IT ASIDE, AND BEGAN HOT-GLUING BUTTONS AROUND THE OUTER SIDES OF THE BOX, USING THE PENCIL MARKS AS A GUIDE. (NOTE:

THE LID WILL NOT FIT IF YOU POSITION BUTTONS ABOVE THE PENCIL LINE.) KIMBERLEY NOTES THAT YOU MAY WISH TO COAT THE BOX AND LID WITH A LIGHT LAYER OF CLEAR ACRYLIC SPRAY TO ADD SHEEN. (NOTE: THESE BOXES WERE MADE FROM INEXPENSIVE CHIPWOOD BOXES, BUT ANY STURDY BOX WILL WORK.)

GRAPEVINE BUTTON WREATH

RESISTING THE TEMPTA-
TION TO FINISH THIS WREATH
WITH A GLUE GUN IN 10% OF
THE TIME, DESIGNER
KIMBERLEY ADAMS ATTACHED
THE BUTTONS BY THREADING
them with 4-inch lengths
of brass wire. (Multiple
colors of wire could be
substituted if more color
is desired.) She pulled the
wire through the
grapevine with pliers and
then twisted the wire on
the back side until it was
tight and secure.
"Attaching the buttons
with wire instead of glue,"
Kimberley notes, "enables
you to enjoy cherished
buttons every day without
risking glue damage, as
well as create interesting
clusters and angles."

BUTTON BOOKS

Looking for a way to include her husband in her button crafts, designer Mary Savage sewed buttons onto several inexpensive journals she found in an art supply store. "The buttons came from suspender straps and coats from vintage menswear, so they seemed a natural

for the books." Mary used upholstery thread (quilting thread or embroidery floss would also work) and an embroidery needle to sew on the buttons.

PAPER PLEASURES

Handmade paper artist Claudia Lee loves the textures, colors, and immediacy of papermaking materials. Most of her pieces reflect her fascination with the emotional connections we have with the everyday things we do and the very common objects with which we do them. "I especially love working with domestic images, so buttons are a natural choice." The paper dolls were inspired by friends from the multicultural neighborhood she grew up in, while the teapots remind her of the ritual of serving tea to visiting friends.

When considering surface design techniques, Claudia tends to think of her handmade papers as being just like a delicate fabric. Although the pieces shown here were made from handmade paper, they can be replicated with any quality paper. To begin, trace a shape or image that you

"I ESPECIALLY LOVE WORKING WITH DOMESTIC IMAGES, SO BUTTONS ARE A NATURAL CHOICE."

find attractive and cut it out from a sheet of paper. Next, brush on several coats of clear gloss medium to strengthen the paper.

Claudia's next step is to decorate the paper with color. If you're not an accomplished dyer, this can be done simply by mixing some liquid dye according to the manufacturer's instructions in a spray bottle and spritzing the dye on in light coats. Claudia recommends varying the intensity of the color to create interesting effects, as well as applying more than one color. (Be sure to let each color dry before applying another.)

Next, Claudia embellishes the pieces with smaller paper shapes (a star or zigzags) and then with puff paint. As the last embellishing step, Claudia glues on the buttons. If you plan to display the pieces as wall hangings, mount them with foam core for added sturdiness.

SILVERSMITHED BUTTON JEWELRY

Kathy Gillespie entered the world of jewelry design several years ago when she began making simple button brooches using craft glue as an adhesive. To refine her work and increase its longevity, she began studying silversmithing. Finally, after several months of course work, she was able to successfully set special buttons in silver with stone-setting techniques.

Kathy's favorite buttons include faceted and engraved glass buttons, (especially ones that have been engraved to look like fabric), and silver and gold luster buttons. "The glass buttons were a challenge to work with. The shank is very difficult to remove, and I was really discouraged by how many but-

tons I broke in the learning process. The metal luster buttons are much easier to work with, since the shanks just snip off, and pieces designed with them are popular with my customers because they can be worn with both gold and silver jewelry."

Kathy's jewelry has been well received at shows, and many of her projects are commissioned jobs from people wanting a special jewelry piece made from cherished buttons passed down through their families. "I don't consider myself a good salesperson, but once I start sharing stories and histories about individual buttons, people really listen. My pieces are an emotional purchase because they're all one-of-a-kind works, and

EACH BUTTON HAS A STORY."
KATHY DOES FIND IT HARD
TO PART WITH HER JEWELRY,
AND TRIES TO BUILD TIME
INTO HER PRODUCTION
SCHEDULE TO ENJOY NEW
PIECES BEFORE THEY LEAVE.
"PARTING WITH THE PIECES
IS THE HARDEST PART OF MY
JOB, BUT IT ALLOWS ME TO
BUY MORE SILVER AND MORE
BUTTONS TO MAKE MORE
PIECES, SO I DO IT."

INITIALLY, KATHY
WAS OBSESSED WITH USING
ONLY PERFECT BUTTONS IN
HER JEWELRY. BUT SLOWLY

**"MY PIECES ARE AN
EMOTIONAL PURCHASE
BECAUSE THEY'RE ALL
ONE-OF-A-KIND
WORKS, AND EACH
BUTTON HAS A STORY."**

SHE BEGAN TO ADMIT THAT
IF A BUTTON HAS BEEN
LYING AROUND IN A BUT-
TON TIN FOR A HUNDRED
YEARS, THEN IT'S NOT GOING
TO BE PERFECT, "AND SINCE
I'M WORKING WITH VERY
OLD MATERIALS, IT JUST
SEEMS SILLY TO WORRY
ABOUT A CHIP OR SCRATCH
IN A CORNER."

THESE EMBOSSED BUTTON PAPERS WERE MADE WITH THE BUTTONS ADORNING THE OUTSIDE OF DESIGNER HEATHER ALLEN'S HAND-MADE BOOK ON PAGE XXX, AND WERE ORIGINALLY CONCEIVED OF AS END PAPERS. TO MAKE THE PAPERS, HEATHER PLACED THE BUTTONS IN BETWEEN TWO LAYERS OF MASHED PULP. WHEN THE PULP IS PRESSED TO REMOVE EXCESS WATER, THE SHAPES ARE EMBOSSED INTO THE DAMP PAPER. "IT TOOK QUITE A BIT OF EXPERIMENTING TO GET GOOD RESULTS. BUTTONS THAT WERE TOO THICK JUST DIDN'T WORK AT ALL, WHILE BUTTONS THAT WERE TOO THIN LEFT HOLES IN THE PAPER." HEATHER EMBELLISHED SOME OF THE BUTTONS WITH DECORATIVE THREADS AND FLOSSES.

"A LOVE OF MINE"

ARTIST SHERRI WARNER HUNTER CREATED THIS BUTTON WALL PIECE FOR A THEME EXHIBITION. AS A FORMER PROFESSIONAL SEAMSTRESS, SHERRI ENJOYED WORKING WITH MATERIALS — SUCH AS BUTTONS AND ZIPPERS — THAT WERE FAMILIAR TO HER. "MOVING THESE MATERIALS OUT OF THEIR FUNCTIONAL ROLES AND INTO MORE PLAYFUL, DECORATIVE ONES WAS VERY SATISFYING."

WHEN CREATING A SIMILAR WALL PIECE, SHERRI RECOMMENDS WORKING WITH A PIECE OF FABRIC WIDE ENOUGH TO FIT INTO A LARGE EMBROIDERY HOOP TO KEEP YOUR ENTIRE DESIGN AREA TAUT AS YOU WORK. (IF YOUR FABRIC IS TOO SMALL, YOU CAN BASTE STRIPS OF MUSLIN ON THE EDGES.) BECAUSE SEWING THAT MANY BUTTONS ON IS A TIME-CONSUMING PROJECT, SHERRI ALSO RECOMMENDS DOUBLING THE STANDARD DOUBLED THREAD (TO CREATE FOUR LENGTHS) AND THEN SEWING THROUGH EACH BUTTON JUST TWICE, KNOTTING THE THREAD AFTER EACH BUTTON TO PREVENT FABRIC PUCKERS.

"MOVING THESE MATERIALS OUT OF THEIR FUNCTIONAL ROLES AND INTO MORE PLAYFUL, DECORATIVE ONES WAS VERY SATISFYING."

BUTTON BIRDHOUSE

ALTHOUGH ARTIST SHERRI WARNER HUNTER'S PIECE, *TREE HOUSE #2: BUTTON WOOD*, DEVELOPED FROM A SERIES OF BIRDHOUSES, IT QUICKLY MOVED INTO A MORE SERIOUS CONTEXT, EXPLORING THE HOME AS BOTH AN INNER SENSE OF PLACE AND AS A PHYSICAL, TRANSIENT PLACE. THIS PIECE IS PART OF AN ONGOING SERIES, WITH SOME OF THE HOMES TAKING ON A WHIMSICAL FEEL AND OTHERS MORE SERIOUS. SHERRI CHOSE BUTTONS AS A MATERIAL BECAUSE OF THEIR MOSAIC QUALITY AND THEIR WONDERFUL COLOR RANGE. THE BUTTONS WERE ATTACHED WITH THE SAME SILICONE ADHESIVE USED ON SHERRI'S BUTTON COAT ON THE FOLLOWING PAGE. THE PIECE IS IN THE PRIVATE COLLECTION OF KRISTI HARGROVE.

BUTTON COAT

No, you can't slip it on for a night on the town, but this button coat is a showstopper nonetheless. As a professional seamstress who once did prototype sewing for fashion construction, artist Sherri Warner Hunter saw the coat as a natural form. Perhaps the most amazing attribute of the jacket is its lining. Instead of a traditional fabric such as cotton or silk, the jacket is fully lined with black buttons.

Sherri's biggest challenge in the project was to create the illusion of dancing in the coat's shape. The coat's initial base was formed from chicken wire and then covered with plaster and burlap. The buttons were attached with a silicon adhesive. "The fumes were awful but I was willing to put up with them to achieve the shiny finish I wanted." Entitled *My Coat of Many Colors on Many Colored Coats . . . Thank You Dolly Parton*, the coat is one in a series. Sherri chose to work with buttons because of their wonderful mosaic

INSTEAD OF A TRADITIONAL FABRIC SUCH AS COTTON OR SILK, THE JACKET IS FULLY LINED WITH BLACK BUTTONS.

quality. The coat is in the private collection of Robin and Mark Cohen.

ORNAMENTAL BUTTON COLLAR

ALWAYS INTRIGUED WITH MINIMAL ATTACHMENTS, ACCESSORIES, AND THE WAY THINGS GO TOGETHER, ARTIST SHERRI WARNER HUNTER WAS PLAYING WITH TWISTING WIRE THROUGH BUTTONS, AND THE WIRE/BUTTON 'FABRIC' IT PRODUCED "JUST KEPT GROWING. I'M NOT QUITE SURE WHERE THE IDEA FOR A COLLAR CAME FROM . . . IT SEEMS TO HAVE BEEN DELIVERED." AS SHE CONTINUED WORKING, SHERRI BEGAN SEEING THE COLLAR AS A POSSIBLE ENTRY FOR AN UPCOMING THEME EXHIBITION ENTITLED "JUNGLE LOVE." SHERRI VIEWS THE COLLAR AS A CONTEMPORARY TRIBUTE TO AFRICAN ORNAMENTATION.

RUNE-BUTTON POUCH AND BOOK

BOOKBINDER AND BUTTON LOVER JOYCE ELAINE SIEVERS BELIEVES BOOKS AND BUTTONS HAVE A LOT IN COMMON. "THE FUNCTION OF BUTTONS IS TO ENCLOSE, AND BY THEIR COLOR, TEXTURE, AND SHAPE, THEY ENHANCE WHAT THEY ENCLOSE. BOOKS ALSO ENCLOSE. OPENING A BOOK, ONE PAGE AFTER ANOTHER, IS ALSO A PROCESS OF REVELATION. BUTTONS AND BOOKS SHARE IN THE PROCESS OF UNVEILING THE UNKNOWN." JOYCE HANDCRAFTS THE BUTTONS FROM CLAY, INSCRIBES THEIR RUNE MARKINGS, AND THEN FIRES THEM. JOYCE BECAME INTERESTED IN RUNES WHEN SHE BEGAN EXPLORING CELTIC LORE. THE LANGUAGE OF RUNES WAS WRITTEN, NOT SPOKEN, AND BELIEVED TO HAVE GREAT POWER. THE IMAGES WERE CARVED ON STONES OR SIMILAR OBJECTS AND THEN CAST OR THROWN. THE PATTERNS THEY FORMED WHEN THEY FELL WERE CONSIDERED TO BE "MESSAGES" OF GREAT IMPORTANCE FROM SPIRITS BEYOND THE VISIBLE WORLD.

BUTTON QUILTS

"I must have been a magpie in another life," laments quilt designer Elizabeth Owen. "I just seem so attracted to shiny things like mother-of-pearl and glass buttons." Elizabeth's grandparents owned a small-town department store in Tennessee when she was a child, and she fondly remembers the woman who ran the alterations department who would save fabric scraps and buttons for Elizabeth to play with. "Embellishing my quilts with buttons seems so natural. Weight adds a comforting quality to textiles, which have traditionally been associated with comfort and shelter."

The fabrics in Elizabeth's quilts are usually decorated with several surface design techniques. After the fabric is imprinted and patchworked, Elizabeth begins adding decorative embellishments such as buttons and beads. Instead of designing and executing in two separate steps, Elizabeth likes to let the design evolve, hanging the quilt up on the wall every few days and playing with the next design stage. "Since textiles have both pattern and color, flat, two-dimensional

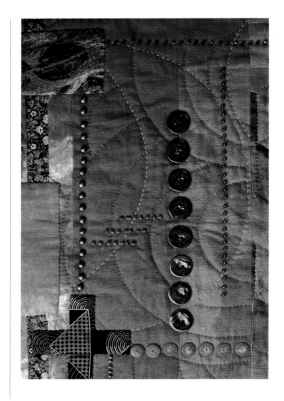

ELIZABETH'S GRANDPARENTS OWNED A SMALL-TOWN DEPARTMENT STORE IN TENNESSEE WHEN SHE WAS A CHILD, AND SHE FONDLY REMEMBERS THE WOMAN WHO RAN THE ALTERATIONS DEPARTMENT WHO WOULD SAVE FABRIC SCRAPS AND BUTTONS FOR ELIZABETH TO PLAY WITH.

drawings are not very helpful in predicting what a finished piece will look like."

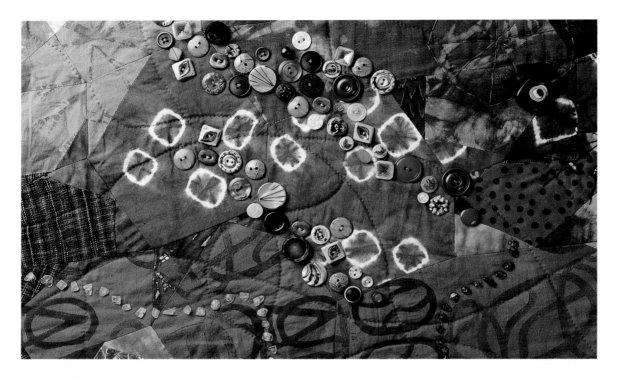

BUTTON FRAME

"Once I started mak-ing button frames," con-fesses crafter Lisa Rhodes, "I had a hard time stopping." Lisa began by hot-gluing a base of inexpensive ivory buttons to a purchased photo frame. Next, she added a layer of special buttons, taking care to position the hot glue away from the sewing holes so the glue wouldn't show through. "Overlapping and layering the buttons creates a really lush look." A coat of clear acrylic spray can be added if desired.

" B L I Z Z I E "

Wᴇɴ ᴍᴜʟᴛɪᴍᴇᴅɪᴀ ᴄᴏʟʟᴀɢᴇ ᴀʀᴛɪsᴛ Jᴀᴄǫᴜᴇ Pᴀʀsʟᴇʏ ʙᴇɢɪɴs ᴀssᴇᴍʙʟɪɴɢ ᴍᴀᴛᴇʀɪᴀʟs ғᴏʀ ᴀ ᴘɪᴇᴄᴇ, ʙᴜᴛᴛᴏɴs ᴀʀᴇ ᴏɴᴇ ᴏғ ᴛʜᴇ ғɪʀsᴛ ᴏʙJᴇᴄᴛs sʜᴇ ᴄᴏʟʟᴇᴄᴛs. "Fᴏʀ ᴄᴏʟʟᴀɢᴇ, ʙᴜᴛᴛᴏɴs ᴀʀᴇ ᴛʜᴇ ᴘᴇʀғᴇᴄᴛ ᴅᴇsɪɢɴ ᴇʟᴇᴍᴇɴᴛ. Tʜɪs ʟɪᴛᴛʟᴇ-ʀᴇᴘᴇᴀᴛᴇᴅ ғᴏʀᴍ sʜᴏᴡs ɪɴᴛᴇʀᴇsᴛ, ᴍᴏᴠᴇ-ᴍᴇɴᴛ, ᴀɴᴅ ʜᴜᴍᴏʀ. Tʜᴇʏ ʀᴇᴘʀᴇsᴇɴᴛ ʟᴏᴠᴇ, ᴡᴀʀᴍᴛʜ, ᴀɴᴅ Mᴏᴍ, ᴀɴᴅ I ʀᴇᴀʟʟʏ ʟɪᴋᴇ ᴛʜᴇ ᴡᴀʏ ᴛʜᴇ ᴄɪʀᴄᴜʟᴀʀ ғᴏʀᴍ ɪɴ ᴀ ʙᴜᴛᴛᴏɴ ʀᴇᴘᴇᴀᴛs ɪᴛsᴇʟғ ᴀɢᴀɪɴ ɪɴ ᴛʜᴇ ғᴏʀᴍ ᴏғ ᴛʜᴇ sᴇᴡɪɴɢ ʜᴏʟᴇs." Jᴀᴄǫᴜᴇ ʙᴇɢᴀɴ *Bʟɪᴢᴢɪᴇ* ᴡɪᴛʜ ᴀ ᴡᴏᴏᴅᴇɴ ʜᴀᴛ ғᴏʀᴍ. Aɴ ᴏʟᴅ ᴘʜᴏᴛᴏ sᴇʀᴠᴇᴅ ᴀs ᴛʜᴇ ᴄᴇɴᴛᴇʀᴘɪᴇᴄᴇ, ᴡʜɪᴄʜ ᴡᴀs ᴛʜᴇɴ ᴇᴍʙᴇʟʟɪsʜᴇᴅ ᴡɪᴛʜ ᴄɪɢᴀʀ ᴡʀᴀᴘᴘᴇʀs, ᴏʟᴅ ᴄᴏs-ᴛᴜᴍᴇ Jᴇᴡᴇʟʀʏ, ᴀ ʀᴏsᴀʀʏ, ᴀssᴏʀᴛᴇᴅ ᴘʀɪɴᴛᴇᴅ ᴍᴀᴛᴇʀɪ-ᴀʟ, ɢʟɪᴛᴛᴇʀ, ᴏɪʟs, ᴘᴀsᴛᴇʟs, ᴀɴᴅ, ᴏғ ᴄᴏᴜʀsᴇ, ʙᴜᴛᴛᴏɴs. "Fᴏʀ ᴍᴇ, ᴄᴏʟʟᴇᴄᴛɪɴɢ ᴛʜᴇ ᴏʙJᴇᴄᴛs ɪs ᴀ ᴠᴇʀʏ ʀᴇᴀʟ ᴘᴀʀᴛ ᴏғ ᴛʜᴇ ᴅᴇsɪɢɴ ᴘʀᴏᴄᴇss."

"THEY REPRESENT LOVE, WARMTH, AND MOM,
AND I REALLY LIKE THE WAY THE CIRCULAR
FORM IN A BUTTON REPEATS ITSELF AGAIN IN
THE FORM OF THE SEWING HOLES."

Clothing designer Carolyn Benforado creates functional, custom clothing for a range of customers, so this dress was a fun departure from her everyday work. "Because of the Coke print, I kept seeing a spray — a 'fizz' — of buttons, and every time I opened the button box and stacked different buttons together it felt like there was a community of buttons dancing all across the fabric."

Carolyn deliberately chose plastic buttons because she saw the dress as a type of Americana, and "plastic buttons seem identifiable as disposable." Sewing the buttons on was a challenge. "They had to be sewn individually so they wouldn't inhibit the fabric's natural stretch. The Lycra fabric

feels very free and liberating. Wearing the dress is almost like body painting, and it looks different on everyone who wears it."

"...EVERY TIME I OPENED THE BUTTON BOX AND STACKED DIFFERENT BUTTONS TOGETHER IT FELT LIKE THERE WAS A COMMUNITY OF BUTTONS DANCING ALL ACROSS THE FABRIC."

"THE ARCHITECTURE WE WEAR"

Textile artist Heather Allen, whose work is often about architecture, is intrigued with the idea that clothing is the house that people wear. "There are building codes, military measurements, and patterns that create 'style,' and buttons are the doorknobs and latches of our cloth houses, being used for both adornment and attachment." Heather surface designed the cloth with fabric and button patterns, and used cut-up sewing patterns for the interior book pages. The book was bound with a buttonhole stitch binding.

▬▬▬ To make a buttonhole bound book you will need a book needle, waxed linen thread, 40 sheets of paper divided into eight groups (called signatures) with five pages each, and a sheet of heavier paper for the cover. Trim the cover paper to measure the same height as the signature sheets and to a length measuring the length of the signature sheets plus additional space for the spine (measure the thickness of your sheets for this measurement) and 3 to 6" of turn-in allowance for front and back flaps.

▬▬▬ Make three cuts to open up a window in the spine and fold back the straps to the inside. Each signature will have two pierced sewing stations slightly inside the area created by the window. There are no holes pierced in the cover or on the very top and bottom of the signature spines; the thread merely wraps around. Determine your thread length by multiplying the length of the spine times the number of signatures. The sewing is done in two sets, across all the top signatures and then across the bottom signatures.

▬▬▬ Begin sewing from the inside of the first signature, leaving a tail to tie with. Take the thread through the hole to the outside and up over the top of the cover's spine tab and down the center of the first signature and tie off inside. Take the needle out and under the first stitch in the opposite direction from the sewing and pull tight.

▬▬▬ Position the next signature. Take the thread through the hole in the second signature to the inside and up the valley to the top. Pull the thread, leaving just enough slack to slip the needle and thread through. Take the thread down the outside and around, and then under the previous stitch. Pull to tighten.

▬▬▬ Position the next signature and repeat the same sewing steps. After the last signature, take the thread to the inside and tie off. Repeat for the bottom the same as the top.

...CLOTHING IS THE HOUSE THAT PEOPLE WEAR.

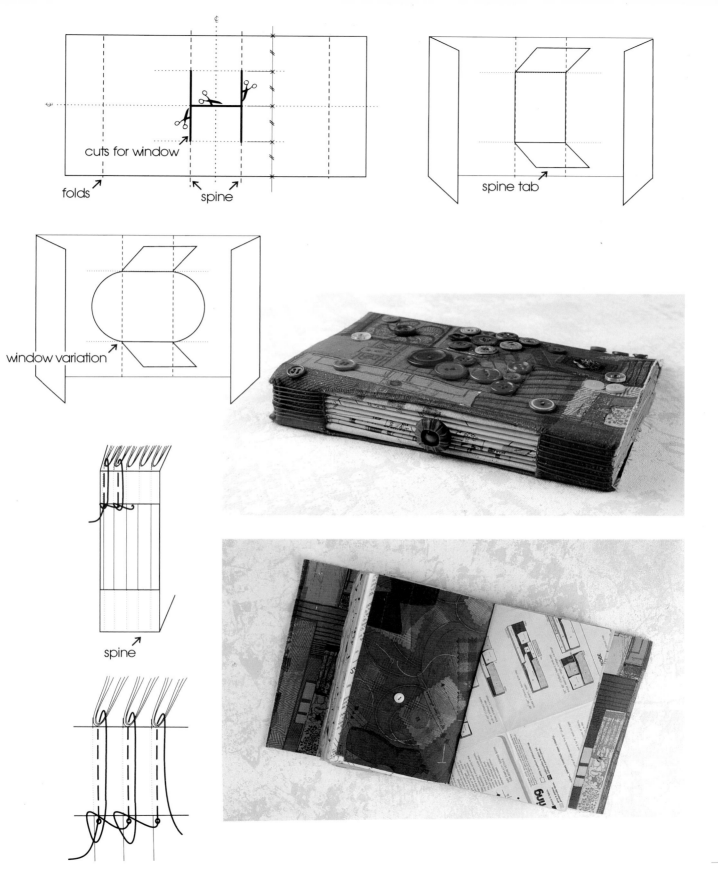

cuts for window

folds

spine

spine tab

window variation

spine

INDEXES

METRIC CONVERSIONS

1/8 INCH	3 MM
1/4 INCH	6 MM
1/2 INCH	13 MM
3/4 INCH	19 MM
1 INCH	2.5 CM
2 INCHES	5 CM
3 INCHES	7.5 CM
4 INCHES	10 CM
5 INCHES	12 CM
6 INCHES	15 CM
7 INCHES	17 CM
8 INCHES	20 CM
9 INCHES	22 CM
10 INCHES	25 CM